THE CIVIL WAR MEMOIR
OF A BOY FROM BALTIMORE

was sunk alongside a pier or rather a wooden wharf, which had been built out into the river 200 or 250 feet, so that steamers could land. The Cumberland's masts arose out of the water quite high and still had the flags and "union jack" flying from them. Not knowing what a most revered, sacred and valuable relics these things were, I undertook one day to get that "Union Jack". I pushed a boat out, and shinned up the mast and after much work in a hot sun I got her and slid down. By this time a big crowd of soldiers were attracted and had been watching me. Someone else had been looking on beside the soldiers, and as soon as I reached the wharf the "Officer of the day" gave me a lecture and said he was ordered to send me back up that mast

and place that "Union Jack" just where I got it from. I re-shinned it up that mast again, and as luck had it, I had not pulled the halyards through the pulley and without very much trouble I got the jack back. Another shout was heard when I saw the flag back and it was a "cold day" when I was not jolted about that climb. By the way a "Union Jack" is a long thin streamer which is seen on all war vessels like this ~~~~~~ The field being blue and one red and white stripe. They are about 15 feet long I should think. I was permitted, when inclined to ride one of the cavalrymens horses, that is when they would let me. One big old and wild artillery horse used to be my favorite, as he attracted attention and I thought I was extra brave when on his back. I would ride him on a walk always

THE CIVIL WAR MEMOIR OF A BOY FROM BALTIMORE

The Remembrance of George C. Maguire
Written in 1893

Edited by Holly I. Powers

Foreword by David Price and Jake Wynn,
National Museum of Civil War Medicine

Voices of the Civil War
Michael P. Gray, Series Editor

Knoxville / The University of Tennessee Press

The Voices of the Civil War series makes available a variety of primary source materials that illuminate issues on the battlefield, the home front, and the western front, as well as other aspects of this historic era. The series contextualizes the personal accounts within the framework of the latest scholarship and expands established knowledge by offering new perspectives, new materials, and new voices.

Frontispiece: Page from original memoir of "Geo C. Maguire, Jr."

Library of Congress Cataloging-in-Publication Data

Names: Maguire, George C., 1847–1908, author. | Powers, Holly I., editor.

Title: The Civil War memoir of a boy from Baltimore : the remembrance of George C. Maguire written in 1893 / edited by Holly I. Powers.

Other titles: Remembrance of George C. Maguire written in 1893

Description: First edition. | Knoxville : The University of Tennessee Press, [2021] | Series: Voices of the Civil War | Includes bibliographical references and index. | Summary: "This memoir recounts the experiences of George Maguire (1847–1908) as a noncombat member of the Fifth Maryland Infantry Regiment. The memoir has two unique features. First, Maguire witnessed and recounts some pivotal events—including the battle of the Monitor and the Merrimac, the battles of the Peninsula Campaign, and Antietam—and his remembrances constitute one of the few memoirs from a Maryland unit. Second, at the outbreak of the war, he was only fourteen years old and ineligible to enlist; however, he served as the Fifth's "mascot" and undertook heavier duty as his service continued. The memoir presents a unique opportunity to examine the experiences of a child during the war and to explore issues of memory"— Provided by publisher.

Identifiers: LCCN 2020051258 (print) | LCCN 2020051259 (ebook) | ISBN 9781621903352 (cloth) | ISBN 9781621903369 (pdf) | ISBN 9781621906483 (kindle edition)

Subjects: LCSH: Maguire, George C., 1847–1908. | United States. Army. Maryland Infantry Regiment, 5th (1861–1865)—History. | United States—History—Civil War, 1861–1865—Personal narratives. | Maryland—History—Civil War, 1861–1865—Personal narratives. | United States—History—Civil War, 1861–1865—Children. | Children and war—United States—History—19th century. | Baltimore (Md.)—Biography.

Classification: LCC E512.5 5th .M34 2020 (print) | LCC E512.5 5th (ebook) | DDC 973.7/452—dc23

LC record available at https://lccn.loc.gov/2020051258
LC ebook record available at https://lccn.loc.gov/2020051259

To those whose ancestors served
in the Maryland Fifth Infantry Regiment

CONTENTS

ILLUSTRATIONS

FOREWORD

It is quite possible that nearly everything you think you know about Civil War medicine is wrong. The belief that surgeons hacked off limbs at every turn, patients bit down on bullets to deal with the pain of surgery, and soldiers were left to fend for themselves after an operation, seems to be the prevailing myth. Nothing could be further from what actually happened. This is why the story of George Maguire is so important. It is a first-person account of the birth of the modern health care system that transformed American medicine over four years of civil war. What makes his story even more remarkable is that he actually participated in that transformation in many different roles. His experience gives us insight into a well-organized medical system that was formed to deal with a level of casualties and sickness that had never been seen in America.

As shot and shell rained down and bullets ripped through the air, young George Maguire of Baltimore, Maryland, navigated the bloody battlefield at Antietam on September 17, 1862. Only fifteen years old, he was relegated from the unit he accompanied to the front lines of combat near Sharpsburg to the medical teams accompanying the Army of the Potomac on the bloodiest day in American history. This boy witnessed horrible carnage as the broken bodies of soldiers were carried to makeshift field hospitals in barns and houses. He witnessed amputations, smelled the ghastly odors of ruptured bodies, encountered men dead and dying, and even crossed paths with the "Angel of the Battlefield" herself, Clara Barton. Maguire's experience on September 17, 1862, is but one of the many vignettes of his war-time recollections in this volume. Maguire's unique viewpoint as a young boy relatively unencumbered by military responsibility and with a curious frame of mind desirous to see firsthand the history being made all around him make this a powerful perspective on the events of the Civil War and valuable insights into the wartime medical system.

Maguire's remembrances, not just of his battlefield excursion at Antietam, bring forward many of the themes the National Museum of Civil War Medicine discuss every single day. Our mission is to preserve and interpret the medical history of the American Civil War, and we strive to do so from three locations—the National Museum of Civil War Medicine itself, in Frederick, Maryland; the Pry House Field Hospital Museum at Antietam National Battlefield; the Clara Barton Missing Soldiers Office Museum in Washington, DC. Our organization is dedicated to telling the story of the medical personnel and the patients who faced treatment for illnesses and wounds in an era just on the eve of many radical medical advancements.

Maguire participated in and witnessed many of the subjects we discuss in depth at the National Museum of Civil War Medicine. How were recruits medically screened? What were conditions like for soldiers serving at the front lines? What was their diet? What sorts of preventative treatments did doctors employ in advance? How were soldiers treated once they became ill in this era before a full understanding of disease and infection was available?

Maguire provides us with a child's eye view of these issues in camp and how he and his comrades faced them. While these challenges were often grim, we discover many sprinklings of the mischief he made while attached to the 5th Maryland Volunteer Infantry (US) in places like Fortress Monroe, Virginia and Point of Rocks, Maryland. His boyish desire to witness the dramatic events around him gave him the courage to witness dramatic and frightening moments. On the streets of his native Baltimore, he observed the aftermath of the Civil War's first bloodshed in the Pratt Street Riot of April 1861. He observed the building of the famed Army of the Potomac on the Virginia peninsula in the spring of 1862. He arrived the day after two ironclads famously dueled in Hampton Roads and beheld their smoking ruins. He saw, too, the black refugees pouring out from Confederate positions, seeking freedom from slavery beyond the lines of the United States Army.

But it was his experience at Antietam on September 17, 1862, that provides vivid descriptions of the military medical realities of the Civil War. After being ordered to accompany his regimental surgeon away from the lines of battle, Maguire became lost in the confusion. He bounced back and forth behind the lines and to the battlefront where his family and friends were fighting Confederates in an engagement that left nearly 23,000 men dead or maimed. He did not know it at the time, but he was witnessing a military medical revolution in action on that horrible day. Major Jonathan Letterman's innovative ambulance and hospital directives had just been put in place by the Army of the Potomac for the very first time. Maguire unknowingly became an active participant in the new system when he joined two wounded soldiers on their trudge from the battlefield at Antietam more than twenty-five miles to the railroad head at Frederick, Maryland, and ultimately to a train bound for their hometown in Baltimore. Through these often traumatic experiences, Maguire's recollections reveal how a young man processed the horror and bloodshed he had witnessed. It left a life-long mark on him, as it did on millions of other Civil War soldiers. His musings on the shocking death of a boy little older than himself on the Antietam battlefield makes this crystal clear.

Even after Maguire goes home to Baltimore, the Civil War and its medical consequences came to him. Still a teenager, he joined the medical staff at the newly constructed Hicks General Hospital on the western end of Baltimore. In the city that saw the first bloodshed of the war, its railroad and shipping connections made it the perfect place for a general hospital to be constructed by the US Army in order to manage the immense casualties of battle and the victims of disease. Here, Maguire played a part in yet another system of battlefield medical care revolutionized by the Civil War. Cities became hospital centers where casualties were transported from the battlefield for long-term convalescence.

Maguire, with his sense of adventure and desire to assist in the Union war effort, gives the reader a glimpse into what it was like to work on the wards of a large military hospital. The sights and smells of the hospital are described. He provides insightful observations on the roles of the personnel, as well as on the size and shape of the hospital itself. Maguire grapples with death, originally fearing the dead bodies that often piled up around him. But he, like countless others during the Civil War, became inured to the suffering, carnage, and destruction all around them.

This volume is an incredibly valuable contribution to our understanding of the Civil War and wartime medicine. In its pages are numerous accounts of medical advancement and how it was experienced by those who were wounded and sick. Through the wondering eyes of a young boy, the war's brutal realities, harsh truths, and bloody consequences are clearly manifest.

At the National Museum of Civil War Medicine, we endeavor to discover new primary sources that provide perspectives on what it was like to live through and provide medical care at the time. This unique memoir provides personal insight on the changes to those practices that set the stage for revolutions in American medicine and ultimately the world. George Maguire opens a window into the past with his clear language and his vivid recollections, allowing modern readers a chance to gaze upon the war's realities and see how average people faced the immense challenges before them. His boyish candor and plain-spoken description make this remembrance particularly poignant. In the years to come, this volume will play an important role in the museum's interpretation, giving our visitors a first-person account of the Civil War and Civil War medicine.

David Price
Executive Director
National Museum of Civil War Medicine

Jake Wynn
Director of Interpretation
National Museum of Civil War Medicine

PREFACE

The memoir of George C. Maguire is the recollection of a 43-year-old man chronicling his experience as a 14-year-old boy who accompanied the Fifth Maryland Infantry Regiment into the American Civil War. It was written in 1893, and has survived in the safe keeping of the Maguire family for the last 128 years.

George Maguire occupied a position within the regiment that could best be described as that of mascot. His story is not that of a combatant, nor that of an officer. It is not the memoir of a soldier, nor that of a military leader. It is, instead, a story that specifically chronicles the experiences of a boy from Baltimore whose age and position within the regiment provides a unique perspective on life in a war-time army. He enters the conflict as an adolescent, and begins his narrative describing childlike adventures within the context of war. As the narrative (and war) progresses, the nature of the author's adventures change as he makes the transition to manhood in the midst of civil war.

Like many of the memoirs and diaries that have helped to tell the story of the American Civil War, the Maguire memoir enriches our understanding of the war and helps to provide a human dimension to the official war record. It also does something a little different than other primary sources in providing the combined insight of the remembrance of an adolescent experience and that of a non-combatant within the Fifth Maryland Infantry Regiment.

Maguire's narrative takes the reader on a journey beginning in the Peninsula Campaign, carrying on through the Battle of Antietam, and the Union occupation of Harpers Ferry. This short narrative expands the themes of social history to include childhood and youth, the daily lives of soldiers, women in the war, the experiences of slaves in the Union army, southern migratory patterns, trade patterns, Jewish traders in the war, and life inside a Union General Hospital. Interwoven across these themes are glimpses of life in Baltimore during the civil war period.

Parts of the narrative do contribute to military history (such as confirming Union army's movements of the Second Corps at the battle of Antietam). The work as a whole contributes to a broader social history that will prove a valuable resource for teachers, researchers, and both general audiences and academic readers.

I was fortunate to be offered the honor of working on this memoir. The first time I read it I was intrigued. I found George C. Maguire a complex character with a unique story. His literary style reflects pragmatism, sincerity, and a sensitivity that is charming. The self-portrayal as a hero, inherent in some parts of the narrative, is endearing. He captured my imagination, and I was compelled to know more about his story. To accomplish this, I set out to research his experience and to provide the historical background of his narrative.

I have provided this historical background in the form of annotations throughout the work. This was done for two reasons. The first was to confirm the accuracy of his memory and the integrity of the information provided in the memoir. Second, Maguire's brief narrative requires some historical background to the narrative, the historical stage, if you will, on which the recollection of his experiences were taking place. My goal has been to illuminate where he was, why he was there, and the larger forces at play behind his experiences. For many of the experiences described, there is an associated annotation that seeks to reveal the larger picture. I have also included additional suggested historiography for more information on topics of relevance throughout the memoir. While by no means completely reflective of the vast literature and work done on specific topics related to the Civil War, I hope these annotations will serve as starting points for those interested in further investigation on a particular topic or aspect of the Civil War. I ask too for forgiveness in advance for leaving so much great work out. The works citations chosen were those that most closely aligned with the subject referenced in the narrative and that can be easily accessed by both academics and a general reader.

This memoir has been found accurate in detail and chronology with respect to the official war record and existing historiography. It is by no means perfect, and where the narrative does not match the official record, or conflicts with existing historiography, this too is noted. The work has been transcribed with minor edits throughout. Edits include spelling corrections and the modernization of spelling to improve readability. Photographs that relate to or enhance the narrative are also included.

ACKNOWLEDGMENTS

I would like to thank the staff members at the Maryland State Archives, National Archives and Records Administration, National Museum of Civil War Medicine, Maryland Historical Society, and the Enoch Pratt Library for highly professional and gracious assistance.

I would also like to thank Darden Asbury Pyron for introducing me to this memoir and for his unwavering support of my efforts to have it published and therefore included in the historical record for posterity.

INTRODUCTION

The *History and Roster of Maryland Volunteers, War of 1861–5,* Volume 1 chronicles the details about the Fifth Maryland Infantry Regiment, which was raised in Baltimore City at the onset of the American Civil War. The report provides the date the regiment was raised, where the men enlisted from, who enlisted, and describes the movements of the regiment throughout the war. It even goes so far as to total the miles traveled, differentiating mileage between boat travel and marching, and adding up the overall combined distances. In addition to this, the record provides the number of men killed, wounded, and lost to disease or other natural causes.

These details speak volumes about the experiences of the men who made up the Fifth Maryland Infantry Regiment. The number of en-listees and the areas from which they were recruited provide a glimpse of Maryland's overall commitment to the Union. The breakdown of battles the regiment participated in and the chronicle of changing command make clear that this group of soldiers, like the soldiers of both armies, endured unspeakable hardships inherent in the atrocity of war. This information as a whole allows for a broad understanding of what it might have been like to be a soldier in that regiment, but more elusive is an understanding of the daily life and more personal experiences of the soldiers as individuals. Thankfully, fate has pro-vided us with an account that fills in some of these details and pro-vides a window to some of the individual stories that lay between the lines of the Official Record of the War of Rebellion. Fate left to us the memoir of George C. Maguire.

Maguire was fourteen years old when the first shots were fired at Fort Sumter. One year later he accompanied the Fifth Maryland In-fantry Regiment to war. He was still an adolescent who occupied a unique position within the regiment that could best be described as a mascot. In this role he witnessed the war as few others did; an ado-lescent noncombatant traveling with the regiment as the companion of his brother-in-law, Lt. Salome Marsh. He never officially enlisted, never carried a weapon, and never acted in any capacity typical of young recruits in the Union army. His position within the regiment allowed him to maneuver between the overlapping worlds of adolescence and manhood, and the often convoluted lines between officers and enlisted personnel in a wartime army. All the while, he experienced battle and army camp life first hand, and then went on to work as a civilian in one of the great military hospitals in the country.

George Maguire's experiences provide a novel perspective on five major facets of the war: the Pratt Street riot in Baltimore, the Peninsula Campaign, the Battle of Antietam, camp life at Harpers Ferry, and life inside Hicks United States General Hospital. His descriptions of these events enrich the historical record and provide new considerations for the existing historical literature, while revealing the ways in which an adolescent adapted to the war.

George Maguire was born in Baltimore County around 1847. He grew up in the sixth ward with his mother, Julia A. Maguire, and his four sisters, Mary, Sara, Susanna, and Margaret. He had three older brothers as well: Joseph E., John E., and William. His oldest sister, Margaret, married Salome Marsh in 1850 and occupied her own household.[1] By the time the war began, George Maguire lived with Margaret and Salome, an arrangement explained in the memoir as one to provide his sister company as she had yet to have had children of her own. His memoir suggests that his brother-in-law was a staunch Union supporter and neither he nor two of George's older brothers hesitated to enlist when Federal regiments were formed in Maryland. Salome Marsh enlisted in the Fifth Maryland Infantry Regiment organized in Baltimore on September 1861. He took George with him when he left. George's brothers William and Joseph also enlisted as privates in Company B of the same regiment.[2]

Maguire's memoir begins on the streets of Baltimore during the tumultuous times directly following the firing on Fort Sumter. As a slaveholding city, Baltimore was divided in sentiment, and Maryland as a whole was the most important border state in the Union by its proximity to the nation's capital. Following Virginia's secession, the nation apprehensively watched as Maryland struggled with its own allegiances.[3] This tension played itself out on the streets of Baltimore as Rebel and Union sympathizers fought with one another for control of the city. Rabble-rousers sparked the riot on Pratt Street that produced the first casualties of the war, and mob raucousness and violence set the tone across the city until Gen. Benjamin F. Butler secured Baltimore for the Union on May 13, 1861.[4] In the opening section of the memoir Maguire vividly describes the mob scene, sectional violence, and political tension that enveloped the city.

Maguire details his experience of this violence and provides a firsthand account of Rebel cruelty and intimidation. He witnessed the organization of Rebel resistance to Union occupation as Union forces filed through Baltimore on their way to defend the capital. He walked at his brother-in-law's side amid violent protest from those who opposed the Unionist cause. His narrative provides a front-line glimpse of the mob disorder in Baltimore at the onset of the war and the confusion and fear in the city. His own biases are clear as he condemns the Rebel sympathizers as raucous, undisciplined traitors, and he lauds the Union and its supporters.

The unique nature of his memoir captures both the adolescent boy who experienced the event and the middle-aged man who is remembering them firmly on the side of pro-Union political ideology. As the narrative progresses, and he moves with the regiment from the outskirts of Baltimore into the Peninsula Campaign, and then on to the Battle of Antietam, it becomes clear that his political beliefs did not govern his compassion. Like many soldiers throughout history, he begins to acknowledge the humanity of the enemy, a transformation that begins for Maguire at camp on the James River in Virginia.[5]

Lincoln's strategy for winning the war hinged on defeating the Confederate Army in Virginia and capturing the Confederate capital at Richmond. Popular sentiment across the Union called for a march on Richmond, as northern newspapers coined the chant "on to Richmond!"[6] Following the Union defeat at the first Battle of Bull Run on July 26, 1861, Union Gen. George McClellan developed a plan that centered on the strategy of taking the Army of the Potomac southward against the Confederate capital at Richmond by way of the Chesapeake Bay at Fort Monroe. This plan— dubbed the Peninsula Campaign— was the impetus that carried Maguire and the Fifth Maryland out of Maryland and into Virginia and battle.

On March 11, 1862, Maguire and the Fifth Maryland were sent to Fort Monroe. They had spent the first year of the war at Camp Lafayette in Baltimore.[7] Over a period of three weeks, 121,500 men, 14,592 animals, 1,244 wagons and ambulances, 44 artillery batteries and an enormous quantity of equipment and supplies were transported to Newport News, Virginia. There, it formed the basis for a formidable new army in addition to the North Atlantic Blockading squadron already stationed just off the Virginia Peninsula. Maguire's memoir captures the success of the mobilization of forces, stores, and equipment and confirms the existing historical record. Further, his account of his stay on the James River provides examples of a powerful, well-fed force complete with the necessary supplies and equipment of a strong army.

Maguire and the Fifth Maryland made their first camp just under the guns of Fort Monroe, one of the largest coastal forts in America. His unit did not see battle but his memoir records days of fishing and adventures on Chesapeake Bay while the carnage of war surrounded him. Death and destruction were always near. The epic battle of the *Monitor* and the *Merrimac* occurred the week he arrived, leaving the remains of the *Cumberland* and the *Congress* as the historical backdrop to his tales of clam digging and exploring the lower Virginia Peninsula. The burning of the *Merrimac* happened while Maguire camped on the James River, providing a front-line view of a very important event, his recounting of which complements existing accounts.

As the Army of the Potomac marched up the Peninsula, Maguire and the Fifth Maryland camped in Hampton Roads at a comfortable base complete with gymnasium. Although the regiment saw little action at this point, Maguire describes navigating picket lines, and was acutely aware that the enemy was, in fact, nearby. These descriptions provide a new consideration for the existing social history of army camp life. Maguire's experiences here open a window onto the operation of an army out of battle. His adventures illuminate social structures within the army and some of the recreational endeavors of soldiers. In the next phase of Maguire's record, the peaceful camp life disappeared. The soldiers of the Fifth Maryland left the Peninsula in September of 1862 and marched to Antietam, where they confronted the realities of military engagement.

In recounting the regiment's march to Antietam, Maguire's narrative takes a somber turn. The carnage of war lined the roadside as the regiment passed through the aftermath of the battle at South Mountain. The unit marched through the war-torn Turner's Gap on September 15, 1862, and on that same evening Maguire and the regiment camped just east of Antietam Creek. They could hear the sound of booming cannon from Harpers Ferry and the Confederate battery at the line of defense in Pleasant Valley. Meanwhile, food and water grew scarce. His brother-in-law tried to send the boy home, but Maguire managed to return to what became the Fifth Maryland's first big engagement of the war at Antietam. He later found himself caught in the cross-fire of the terrible fight, and if not for good luck and a

quick-thinking surgeon, Maguire may have lost his life on the edge of
Antietam Creek.

On September 16, Maguire recalls spending the day at camp with
the rest of the Army of the Potomac. His narrative recounts the ex-
pectation that the regiment would move into battle that very morning, reaffirming the historical record and providing some insight to
the mindset of the soldiers' pre-battle anxiety. On the morning of the
seventeenth, the Fifth Maryland moved against the rebels and played
a conspicuous role in one of the most famous actions of the battle at
the Bloody Lane. As the regiment fought, Maguire was taken under the
wing of the regimental surgeon, and soon found himself knee deep
in severed limbs and dying bodies at an Antietam field hospital. He
was kept busy assisting with surgical instruments, filling canteens for
the wounded, and making piles of amputated limbs. His memory of
this experience are echoed by other accounts on many levels, but it
also signals the beginning of his particular adaptation to the war. His
descriptions of the manner in which the surgeons and Army Medical
Corps handled the casualties from Antietam, and the networks in play
to facilitate medical care, illuminate some of the reforms of the Army
Medical Corps as the war progressed. His narrative also illustrates additional problems confronting the Medical Corps, such as the ways
in which mental illness and psychological trauma strained an over-
wrought and ill-prepared medical system. A chance encounter with
Clara Barton is also noteworthy and confirmed by other witnesses,
reminding the reader of the emerging presence of women in the field
of medicine.

The Battle of Antietam raged into the night of Wednesday, September 17. On Thursday morning the battle ceased when the Army of the
Potomac was ordered to hold its ground. General McClellan hesitated
once again, and on this day, labeled "fatal Thursday" by one Northern
newspaper, McClellan allowed his battle-worn troops to rest instead
of pushing them on to destroy the Army of Virginia. Meanwhile, the
Confederate forces retreated back into Virginia and a weary and battle-
stunned George Maguire now agreed to return home.

Maguire's stay at home, however, was short-lived. He was restless,
and after finding that he was unable to reacclimatize to school, he
longed to be with the regiment once again. In Maguire's recollections
he rejoined the regiment at Harpers Ferry in December of 1862. Back
with his kinsmen, Maguire memorialized the war-torn town and the
daily life of the Union troops stationed there during this period.

At that time the Fifth Maryland garrisoned the strategic town of Harpers Ferry at the confluence of the Potomac, Shenandoah, and the Chesapeake and Ohio Canal. According to the official war record, the Fifth Maryland moved to Harpers Ferry on September 22, 1862, after the Battle of Antietam. It remained there until January 1863, when the government reassigned it to Point of Rocks and Maryland Heights to protect the Baltimore and Ohio Railroad through June of 1863.[8]

At Harpers Ferry, Maguire's role within the regiment began to shift. While still a boy who found a great deal to amuse him, he also acquired more responsibility. After the regiment shifted to Point of Rocks, he became the unofficial assistant to the provost marshal, his brother-in-law Salome Marsh. His duties included issuing passes for people to cross the Potomac in and out of the Confederacy. His narrative reveals the porousness of the blockade lines, as he tells of encountering a variety of people attempting to provide relief to the Confederacy or escape war-ravaged southern states. Among other things, he describes Jewish traders and southern aristocratic women applying for permission to cross the river. In this way he illustrates the effect of the war on civilians, reveals the types of commodities in demand throughout the South, and describes the migratory routes of war refugees. In addition, his narrative provides examples of the familiar struggle with corruption within the Union ranks.

In June of 1863 the Fifth Maryland was ordered to Winchester, and Maguire left the regiment for the last time. By this time, he was hardened to the realities of what was becoming a seemingly endless struggle. This phase of his record reveals his recognition of how profoundly both he and his home town have changed during the course of the conflict. The next part of his memoir underlines both.

McClellan's' success at Antietam spared Baltimore a Confederate invasion, but it did not spare its inhabitants the consequences of war. After the battle, thousands of wounded were sent to the city for care. Makeshift hospitals appeared wherever there was space to accommodate the influx of the wounded. Overnight "the city had become a vast complex of medical facilities,"[9] according to one authority. Throughout 1863 and 1864, Baltimore continued to be a center for the care of the wounded, with thousands more arriving following the battle of Gettysburg in July of 1863. The Baltimore health-care crisis provided the back drop to Maguire's next course of action.

The Federal government responded to the avalanche of casualties by constructing new hospitals. In 1861, the government had opened the first United States General Hospital in Baltimore. Three more followed in 1862. The last general hospital to be constructed in Baltimore was Thomas Hicks U.S. General Hospital, named after Maryland's first war-time governor. It was located at the intersection of Pulaski Street and Lafayette Avenue in northwest Baltimore and opened in June of 1865.[10] Maguire spent the early days of Reconstruction at this hospital. The battlefield of Antietam and the blockade lines of Harpers Ferry served to provide him with the skills and aptitude to care for the wounded.

The narrative at this point provides a clear depiction of the general structure and layout of the Hicks hospital. Maguire's sketches and diagrams match actual images of the facility, and his explanations of the staffing hierarchy illuminates the operating procedures implemented by the Army Medical Corps at the end of the war. Hicks U.S. General Hospital was in fact a manifestation of all the Army Medical Corps had learned during the conflict. It was a model of the lessons learned in the poor construction of previous hospitals and implemented the designs and systems thought to best facilitate recovery. Maguire's descriptions of ward design and the emphasis placed on nutrition in healing highlight the implementation of practices derived from the lessons of war.

In 1865, Maguire turned eighteen. His first real job as a man found him on the frontlines of a rapidly changing medical field. He witnessed the emergence of new treatments and new discoveries in medicine while he continued to grow and adapt to military exigency. Throughout the narrative his sense of compassion and duty color his words. He provides specific examples of the cases the hospital treated, and some of the options of treatment. His narrative revivifies the experiences of the dying, the wounded, and not least of the care given. This section of the narrative also opens a window on the innovations, accomplishments and failures of the army medical services during the Civil War.

George Maguire's account of his experiences during the early part of the war provides an important discourse on the narrative of that epic struggle. Beyond simply retelling the events as they happened, his memoir is woven with a sense of remorse and resolve, loss, fear, and pure wonderment of a teenage boy accompanying one of the largest assembled armies of its day. His perspective will add to the existing and growing body of work on the history of childhood and youth, especially related to the American Civil War.[11] Also throughout his narrative is a sense of steadfastness and innovation that characterized the armies of the North and rallied its civilians. The very nature of this story, the compassionate theme, and the very practical disposition of his prose push the reader beyond mere description and into the camps and hospitals of the Civil War. In this environment Maguire made the transition from boy to man and acquired the skills to navigate the shifting political, moral, and economic landscape that accompanies war.

Historian Stephen Mintz has written, "in times of war, age lines blur, new demands are made of the young, and a child cannot be insulated from adult realities."[12] The American Civil War was no exception. The memoir of George Maguire substantiates this insight and provides a glimpse into the lives of ordinary youths swept up in the currents of war. It also speaks to the daring bravery exhibited by many adolescents who lived through that epic conflict. As an author Maguire provides posterity with the experience of a boy on the precipice of manhood, a young man growing up in the midst of civil war, whose adolescent exploits while living among soldiers and battle humanize the experience of war and all of its atrocities. The uniqueness of his position and age allows for the consideration of new questions in existing discourses and complements the current literature. Most importantly though, this memoir opens a window to a new history that seeks to consider the ways in which adolescents adapt to war.

CHAPTER 1

FROM BALTIMORE
TO THE PENINSULA CAMPAIGN
WITH THE FIFTH MARYLAND
INFANTRY REGIMENT

I was about 12 years of age when the first gun was fired on Fort Sumter. I can remember of hearing my brother-in-law, who was a most rabid Abolitionist talk about what was going on, but I gave only a casual hearing to what was said, thinking more about getting my lessons and play than about war.

During the campaign of Bell & Everett, Lincoln & Hamlin etc., the processions on the eve of the election for the former and the Democrats were immense.[1] I can remember how the full rigged vessels, manned by boys rigged out as sailors, and the monuments towering so high that the tops were hinged so as they could be lowered when passing under wires.[2]

Baltimore City was a rebel city. That is, a majority of its citizens favored the south and when the war first began a great majority were secessionists.[3] Most of those too ignorant to know what the war was for, or what the cause was for it, followed the crowd. The mob favored anything for excitement.

When the little band of "Republicans" or "Lincoln Men" or as they were called in Baltimore, "Black Abolitionists" concluded to parade before the election they were persuaded not to try it.[4] They were told that the other parties would mob them, but about 150 turned out one evening with oilcloth capes and caps and lanterns.[5] I followed the parade and was with my brother-in-law. He tried his best to get me to go home, but I was afraid after getting a distance away, so I followed along with an umbrella in my hand, as it was cloudy. Just before we came to the Bellaire Market House,[6] my brother-in-law handed me his lantern while he fixed some of his belongings and I was still arranging the lantern when we came opposite the market. In the shadow I saw a large crowd, and when our little parade was all in front of this crowd, someone yelled, "Now! Let them have it." I saw the men drop. Lanterns were bursted by stones and bricks and while wondering what the trouble was, "bang" my head felt as if a steam car was pushing through it, and something wet was running all over my face and down my neck. I drew my hand over my face, looked at what it collected and saw blood. I fainted and when I came around I was lying in a drug store. I remember, when the rocks first began to fly, seeing my brother-in-law draw a great big revolver and yell "Lets clear them out," (he was a brave man and feared nothing) but many of our men were cowards and ran. Of course the procession quit going any further, and no more parades were undertaken by the men who intended on voting for Lincoln.

The next thing I remember was hearing that Abe Lincoln "The Black Abolitionist" had been elected, but he would never be President. He would never be allowed to take the office, nor even get to Washington. He would be killed first.[7]

Then came the news that Lincoln was in Washington and had gone through in disguise.[8]

Then came the talk of war.[9] I can only remember indistinctly of war and secession of this, that and the other state and the talk about Maryland seceding. Red, white and red flags, neck ties, badges, and palmetto and rattlesnake flags were thick in Baltimore.[10] It seemed to me that everybody nearly wore a rebel design of some kind. Even those who were afterwards strong Union people were parading a rebel badge.[11]

My brother-in-law with many other abolitionists were ordered to leave the city, a notice being received by each.[12] My old school teacher received a notice and left, but my brother-in-law remained and let it be known that if anyone wanted him to leave they should come and inform him personally and when they came, to come prepared. No one was courageous enough to come and so he remained.

I took no account of what was going on, only as I saw the pictures in the papers in the front of the stores, until the 19th of April. I was down towards the Philadelphia depot and met a boy friend. "Oh," said he, "They have just had an awful fight up on Pratt Street between soldiers and people. Lot's killed! Let's go up." And boy-like, away we went. Trains coming from Philadelphia and going south have to be pulled through one of the busiest streets of the city. The pulling is done by trained horses. When we got onto this street (Pratt Street) I saw the car track had been torn up in places, piles of lumber were high across in other places, and wagons loaded with everything with the wheels off were also across the tracks. In fact so much stuff was piled on this street and across the tracks that wagons could hardly get along the street. We listened to the talk of people who were telling how the mob pelted the soldiers with rocks and fired at them and then in turn the soldiers fired at the mob, and the number killed and so on.[13] Well, when the rest of the scalawags heard about the fight they gathered in thousands and all went down to the depot determined that no Northern soldiers should ever pass through Baltimore. As soon (that day) as a train came in filled with soldiers, the mob ordered them back and they went back. Only one or two trains came in. I suppose others were notified. The train I saw was of box cars with wooden seats or benches made of rough boards. The soldiers were eating a lunch as they came in, but when they saw the mob and heard their cries, they undoubtedly lost their appetites, as I saw most of the lunches were left behind. [See fig. 1 and fig. 2.]

Fig. 1. Massachusetts Militia passing through Baltimore, 1861. Published by Virtue & Co. Publishers, N.Y. F.O.C. (Felix Octavius Carr) Darley and F. F. Walker. Hambleton Print Collection, Special Collections Department. Courtesy of the Maryland Historical Society, item ID # H254.

Fig. 2. First blood. The Sixth Massachusetts Regiment fighting their way through Baltimore, April 19, 1861. Medium Prints Collection, Special Collections Department. Courtesy of the Maryland Historical Society.

I think that about two-thirds of the mob who were wild in driving these few men back to Philadelphia or outside of Baltimore did not fully know what they were doing it for. And that fully that number of them afterwards became Union soldiers themselves. I had no idea what it was all about then.

There was great excitement in the city all that day and night and the next day and night. It was at this time that all abolitionists were ordered to leave, my brother-in-law with them. On the south of Baltimore about 3 miles, at the mouth of the Patapsco River is Fort McHenry. There was much talk of capturing it. Why they didn't I do not know. On the south of the harbor, almost in the center of the city is a very high hill the bluff on the city side. This hill is called "Federal Hill." Well, on the third morning of this mob, when the people awoke, they found a regiment of red-legged "Zouaves" [sic] had charge of this high hill overlooking the city. Cannon had been planted there and the order from the Commandant (who was General Benjamin. F. Butler) to the mayor was that if any more troops were molested or interfered with, he would bombard the city.[14] Then the scenes changed. All the ignoramuses became adherents of the red-legged soldiers and in a few days the Union soldiers had no better friends anywhere than the same mob who had been ready such a short while back to almost "cut them alive." [See fig. 3 and fig. 4]

Then came news of different young men we knew enlisting in the Union Army, and others going south to enlist in the Confederate Army. I had three brothers-John, Joseph and William. John the oldest went out to camp to enlist for three months. Tried it one night and got enough. He came home in the morning, having had soldiering sufficient to last him through the war.

One day my brother-in-law came home (I should have stated that I was living with my brother-in-law, having been taken by my sister as company, she never having any children of her own) and stated a friend of his was going to raise a company for the 5th Maryland Regiment and wanted him for 1st Lieutenant. After much talk it was settled and the company was soon raised and went into camp on the outskirts of Baltimore. My two brothers Joe and Bill joined this company.[15]

I was most of the time in camp with my brother-in-law. My sister made me a regular soldier's suit of clothing and I considered myself one of them. The regiment remained in this camp for nearly a year.

Fig. 3. Federal troops on Federal Hill, looking northwest. Glass negative by David Bachrach (1845–1921) or William Henry Weaver (1825–1913), ca. 1862–1865. Baltimore City Life Museum Collection. Courtesy of the Maryland Historical Society, item ID: CC969.

Fig. 4. South side of the [Baltimore] harbor, ca. 1862–1865. Baltimore City Life Museum Collection. Courtesy of the Maryland Historical Society, item ID # CC987.

They had a brass band and 24 drums and used to parade through the city in grand style. I was told the object was to catch more recruits.

Well one day in September word came to prepare to embark for Newport News, Virginia.[16] The Merrimac—a fearful war boat[17] was building at Norfolk by the rebels, and in case she was as formidable as supposed, troops must be in the neighborhood so we marched away to the wharf, got on a big steam boat and the next day was landed at Newport News, Virginia, on the James River, 6 miles below, and in sight of Fort Monroe. My mother and sisters and nearly all the relatives of all the men were at the wharf to see us off, and many tears were shed then, and I expect many more before many of these men returned.[18]

CHAPTER 2

SUMMER ON THE
VIRGINIA PENINSULA

But what a sight greeted us at Newport News. A few days before, three war vessels fully armed and manned were lying at this place. A long wooden pier extended out into the river, and alongside of this pier the large wooden war ship *Cumberland* was moored. Anchored about 100 yards away on the other side of this pier was the *Congress*, another war vessel. I think there was another, but I am not certain. Anyhow, when we arrived in the morning and embarked onto this pier, the *Cumberland* was at the bottom of the river, the masts only rising above the water alongside the pier, and the *Congress* was burned to the water's edge and was still smoking. It was a sight long to be remembered. Nearly every man of each and both vessels were lying at the bottom either killed or drowned.[1]

It appears that the morning before, the *Merrimac*, which had been finished by the Rebels, put out from Norfolk and at once steamed down to New Port News where these vessels were lying having no idea what an awful fate would soon be that of those on board. They saw her coming and I suppose they hardly knew what she was outside of thinking whatever it was they were fully able to not only "knock her galley west" but to capture her beside.[2]

Down she steamed only two miles to come. Looking exactly like a shed floating on the water all sunk but the roof. She pulled around alongside the *Cumberland* and called for her to surrender. I would think the commander of the *Cumberland* smiled at such a proposal although his vessel was broadside against the pier, with no steam on, or not enough to move her, and only the one side of his vessel could be used. A broadside from the *Cumberland* was the reply, but the shot was as harmless to the *Merrimac* almost as so many peas. They struck her inclined roof of railroad iron and glanced off over the top doing no harm at all. Not so with the Cumberland. The Merrimac had sent into her side solid shot of death and destruction. Another request for surrender "Never," shouted the Captain "We'll go down with the Cumberland." It was foolishness and a sacrifice of the lives of his men. The Merrimac passed alongside with another broadside, described a circle and came at the Cumberland bow on. An immense ram protruded from her bow and with a full head of steam on, she sunk this ram deep into the side of the Cumberland and then backed away. It was all over soon. Those that could escaped, but scores "went down with the Cumberland." After finishing the Cumberland she turned her attention to the Congress, which had not yet been able to get up sufficient steam to move. It was a like fate and the Congress was soon a burning wreck. It is said that the Congress and the Merrimac were commanded by brothers by the name of Buchanan.[3] I do not know how true it is. [See fig. 5.]

Fig. 5. U.S. frigate Cumberland, 54 guns—the flag ship of the Gulf Squadron, Com. Perry. Lith. & pub. by N. Currier, 152 Nassau St. cor. of Spruce N.Y., [1848]. Print shows the U.S. frigate Cumberland port side view under full sail. The ship was eventually sunk in 1862, during the U.S. Civil War, when rammed in a battle with the recommissioned ironclad CSS Virginia, formerly the USS Merrimac. Library of Congress.

After destroying the *Congress* the *Merrimac* headed for Fortress Monroe, surrounding which was a whole fleet of government vessels which the *Merrimac* intended and could have cleaned out like so many cracker boxes but "what's this thing in the way?" "By jove! Here's a cheese box on a raft standing right at us, give her a shot gunner and send her to the bottom cheese and all." "Why here what's this?" Why up boys! Here a queer craft." And it was. The little *Monitor* had arrived just in time. There is no telling how much damage the *Merrimac* would have done to the government fleet had the *Monitor* not disabled her in this set-to. The *Merrimac* instead of sinking every vessel about Fort Monroe was so badly crippled that it was as much as she could do to get back to Norfolk.[4] The Captain of the *Monitor* was blinded during the fight by some iron splinters getting into his eyes; else it would have been up with the *Merrimac* then and there. The *Merrimac* having got the worst of it steamed into Norfolk. [See fig. 6.]

When our Regiment arrived at Newport News they were marched back from the river about one quarter mile or so and went into camp. The river along here had a high bank on bluff extending along for two miles or so, and a beach of about 40 feet. It was impossible for a

Fig. 6. The *Monitor* and *Merrimac*. Library of Congress.

vessel on the river to fire a ball directly at our camp, but there was a chance to shell us. So when there was any possibility of the camp being shelled we would get close to the bluff which gave us protection.

The afternoon of our arrival and while the regiment was laying out and pitching their tents I went looking around. I remember there was box after box of cartridges lying all over. There was a level stretch of ground here extending about a ½ mile back from the river and maybe some two miles or more along it. Beyond this was timber and swamp and then level and so on. Seeing all these cartridges going to waste, I at once got a pile of them, took out the balls, built a fire and melted them, and making a mold of a tomahawk in the ground I soon had a leaden tomahawk. This old tomahawk went the rounds and finally landed in Baltimore and may be at my brother-in-law's home there yet for all I know.

Every few days the Merrimac would steam out of Norfolk and run up to nearly opposite to where we were encamped. The news would soon be spread that the Merrimac was out, and hundreds would go up to the bank of the James River both to see what she was going to do and to get out of reach of any shells she might throw. When the news was heralded that the Merrimac was out "she is going to shell us," was always put to it, and I was afraid of shells. I was always particular to be up near the bank when she was out and of course had a good view of her. There was a few cannon mounted on this bluff inside a kind of fort and when the Merrimac was doing such havoc with the Cumberland and Congress this little fort kept up a constant fire at her. The Merrimac tried to silence them but her balls went over the bank, and I found hole after hole where a cannon ball had sunk into the earth, and a bigger and wider depression once in a while where a shell had exploded and dug up the earth.

The Merrimac always came out in the evening. After tea I guess. One afternoon-an exception to the rule —she came out about 3 p.m. I cannot tell the date, but she steamed down opposite Newport News and turned and went back a mile or so, came back opposite our camp again and then returned and ran up towards Fort Monroe. It looked to me as if she ran within a couple hundred yards of the vessels that were anchored about the Fortress, of which there were perhaps 50 or more of all kinds. After getting that near she turned again and steamed direct into Norfolk. A big wooden steamer followed after her and was within 100 yards of her until she disappeared. All this time she never fired a shot. Whilst this steamer was seemingly chasing her and trying to get her to turn and show fight, I saw a little insignificant looking raft with a big round turret on it put out from among the vessels lying around the fort and cross over and get behind a wooded point of land opposite the fort. I then saw why a wooden steam boat was chasing after such a supposed formidable monster as the Merrimac. The Monitor was anxious for a chance to engage her again, and the wooden boat was trying to get her to turn and show her fight, when the Monitor would have got between her and Norfolk and then one or the other would have gone to the bottom. But she didn't turn and this was the last daylight view we ever had of the Merrimac.[5]

That same night, or next morning, I think about 2:00 a.m., I heard there was a vessel on fire off the flat point of Newport News and opposite Norfolk harbor. I lost no time getting into my clothing and down to the point which ran out into a flat swampy beach. Out about the middle of the mouth of the James River, which was about two miles wide, was something on fire. It was dark all about, but out there the flames were pouring out some small square holes which we took for port holes. We soon saw as the flames shot out that it looked like the Merrimac and some onlookers were certain of it. "It is the Merrimac; she is on fire at the bow." I watched the fire for a half an hour or so. Then something seemed to explode which sounded as if cannon had exploded. Someone said "the gun on her forward part bursted." The blaze shot out high and bright after this and it must have been an hour or so after when there was a terrible explosion and the whole river seemed to heave and was lit up brightly. Then all died out and the darkness was intense. "The Merrimac is no more," was yelled and whooped and hollered as the watchers returned to camp. The lazy ones were awakened, told the news and then permitted to snooze again.[6]

It was certainly a relief to many. It was a common report to hear that the "Merrimac was coming out tonight to shell the camp." Of course no one knew if it was to be done, or where the report came from, whether it was official or otherwise. We never knew at what time of night a big shell would burst beside us, and send us into eternity, but it didn't.

We arrived at Newport News the next morning after the Merrimac sunk the Cumberland and sunk and burned the Congress. For a week or ten days afterwards the dead would be continually washed up on the beach. Morning after morning would a dead body be picked up on the sands and soon the fife and drum would be heard playing the dead march on its way to the grave. All around this part of Virginia the waters were full of crabs, and every poor sailor that was washed ashore had his face and every other part of his body these crabs could reach eaten off or partly eaten off.

There was a line of pickets always kept out on the land side of our camp, as it was feared the "rebs" might come in that way and take us by surprise. I found the pickets in this way. Someone captured a young pig and gave it to me. I kept it tied in my tent, when my brother-in-law and I lived together. One day Mr. Pig got loose and struck out on a fine gallop for the timber. I saw him going and gave chase. I followed him for over a mile, but to no purpose, he was a regular wind-splitter and kept on after I was run out. I started back to camp but was stopped by a picket. How I passed the line going out I do not know but I was captured and taken into camp. The officers wondered much about how I got out beyond the pickets without being seen.

When the army of the Potomac under General McClellan started for Richmond via the Peninsular [sic], they were brought to the Fortress Monroe (a great many of them) and a big camp was established about two miles from our camp. They were fitted out at this camp before going forward.[7] So long as this great body of soldiers was out there, we never saw one of them. In marching to the fort they had the idea (I think) that they were far out into wild Virginia and not anywhere near another camp. I had heard they were out there, so one day I went out. I passed our pickets and went on and finally reached the camp. But not a living soul was to be seen. Here's where they were, but had disappeared, "Marched on." They had occupied a large space. All about were evidences of the waste of war. Barrels of vinegar, molasses, sugar, salt, coffee, and crackers, in fact all kinds of food in abundance was piled up or scattered about in ruthless waste. Here was a pile of brass epaulets-probably a big wagon load—which had been issued to the soldiers to be by them sewed on their shoulders. They seemingly thought they were more for show than use, so they had "re-issued them," by every man throwing them into the same heap. A box, part full of clothing, underwear, shoes, everything that went to outfit an army was out there in the wilds of Virginia, thrown away. Oh! What a waste! I was wonder-struck, and could but think that someone must be here to guard all this stuff. But no, it was all due the men who had passed on. They were charged with it and it was their loss. Poor fellows! Many of them never returned, and car after car load were brought back to the fort in a few months, wounded and dying.[8]

After walking about through this place for a while, I went on further and saw a house away over there on the banks of the James River and I thought I would go over and get acquainted. It was a big house, with beautiful surroundings and about 50 yards from the river. A broad lane ran down between overhanging branches of immense tress to the river. Here was a small wharf and one only flat bottom boat. I went up to the big house, and partly around it, came back and rapped. No one seemed to be about. I knocked and pounded and finally went in through a window, although every other door—except the front door was unlocked. Not a soul was about. Nearly all the furniture was there. Nice old time stuff. Much was out of place and turned about as if the people had left in a hurry. After looking around, trying the piano—which seemed intact, I began to think where I was: three miles from camp, two miles from the nearest picket and in a place where it was none of my business to be. There might be hundreds of rebels all about. The owner of the house might even now be watching me with a rifle at his shoulder, and all though I was but a 13 year old boy, yet they might take me for a spy, as I was surely spying about. I knew there were rebels on the other side of the river, for they had a fort over there, and with a glass we could see their red, white, and red flag, and I did not know, but some of them came across once in a while and might even now be foraging about these very places.

It was a warm day, almost noon, and the sun was extra hot, and I longed for a conveyance back to camp. The boat! I went down and looked at it. It was old and rickety, but I had been in worse ones. An old mast was there. I went back to the house and got an old fashioned Dutch counterpane and brought it down and fastened it to the mast. I found an old home-made oar and after getting a couple of barrels of water bailed out of the boat, I pushed out in the stream and headed for camp. The wind was dead in the rear and the old Dutch counterpane filled out in great slope and I was as proud as if I had captured a gun boat. I was well out in the stream when I passed our picket. I could just hear him shout, and then a musket ball came ricocheting over the water, but not very near. I had been ordered to halt. The picket could not see who I was. Once in a while a deserter would come over from the rebs in this way, and I guess he thought I was one of them and wanted the honor of making the capture. But I was bound for camp, and to camp I was going. I got opposite the rebel fort when "bang!" "Whew!" A cannon ball passed me 25 yards ahead, another and another "bang, bang!" I suppose it was that old counterpane that caused a wonder and attracted so much firing. But they couldn't hit me, and on I went. When I got near enough to see our beach, I saw that the

Fig. 7. Ships on the James River, ca. 1861–1869.
Library of Congress.

bluff, the beach and the pier was black or I might better state, blue with soldiers. All curious to find out what this was coming. It is pretty hard to think what the thoughts of many were at such a craft. I finally reached the beach, ran the bow of the boat up on the sand. General Mansfield[9] and a dozen or more big officers were there. Everyone was silent until I got up and jumped out. The General lifted his hands as if in amazement and when they saw who it was such a shout went up as was ever again heard at Newport News and never before. The General knew whose boy I was and sent for my brother-in-law and I came near having to retire. I told the General there was a boat he could have, but he never used it, and the last I remember it was used as a mark for soldiers to shoot at in practice. [See fig. 7.]

One thing I regretted was an accident that occurred just as the men were shouting. A bank gave way on the bluff and precipitated about 20 men to the beach below, about 20 or 30 feet. A number were badly bruised and a Negro had an arm broken. As he was a Negro cook I had had a quarrel with I did not care so very much and he got well in a short time.

These were happy, careless days for me, but like all young people, I have no doubt I would like to have made frequent changes. No one is ever contented. I was not by any means a bad or even mischievous boy, yet I got myself into frequent unpleasant predicaments. As I have before stated the Cumberland was sunk alongside a pier or rather a wooden wharf, which had been built out into the river 200 or 250-feet, so that steamers could land. The Cumberland's mast rose out of the water quite high and still had the flags and Union Jack flying from them. Not knowing what a most revered, sacred, and valuable relics these things were I undertook one day to get that Union Jack. I pushed a boat out, and shimmed up the mast and after much work in the hot sun I got her and slid down. By this time a big crowd of soldiers were attracted and had been watching me. Someone else had been looking on beside the soldiers, and as soon as I reached the wharf the Officer of the Day gave me a lecture and said he was ordered to send me back up that mast and place that Union Jack just where I got it from. I re-shimmed it up that mast again, and as luck had it, I had not pulled the halyards through the pulley and without very much trouble I got the Jack back. Another shout was heard when I ran the flag back and it was a "cold day" when I was not joked about that climb. By the way a Union Jack is a long thin streamer which is seen on all war vessels like this [see fig. 8] the field being blue and one red and white stripe. They are about 15 feet long I should think.

Fig. 8. Union Jack sketch by George Maguire.

I was permitted when inclined, to ride one of the cavalrymen's horses, that is, when they would let me. One big old and wild artillery horse used to be my favorite, as he attracted attention and I thought I was extra brave when on his back. I would ride him on a walk always up over this level strip (which was as level as a floor for about two miles or more and from a ¼ to a ½ mile in width on one side of the river and the other a marshy and thick forest). One evening I was prancing along and had got close besides the tent of some soldiers when a loud and sudden toot from a horn or bugle scared the big old fellow, and away he went. I hung on as long as I could-about 200 yards and then tumbled off. A hundred men ran to pick me up, but I wasn't hurt the least, which surprised them all, and was on my feet in a few seconds and watching the old horse cantering as fast as he could for the next county. I never saw him again and suppose he kept on until picked up by some rebel, nor did we have to pay for him. I guess he was marked "dead" on the Quartermasters books—with whom we were well acquainted and who messed with our mess.

The timber here was full of briar root of which tobacco pipes are made of and I have seen most beautiful pipes and other small articles made by the soldiers out of this root.

I intended to mention that after visiting the camp, where so many articles were going to waste, I made it known, and the following Sunday a great number got passes and went out. These soldiers picked up lots of things and expressed them to their homes. Very few civilians were at Newport News at this time.

I left my fine suit of soldier clothes at home when I left and was wearing a suit of what was then called in Baltimore "Confederate Gray." The coat was double breasted. Soon I had all the fine buttons off of it, and in their place I had sewed soldier buttons. I had a lot of Maryland buttons and would exchange with soldiers from other states for their state buttons, and I had gathered sufficient to have every button a different one.[10] I was a boy. I took no account of time and therefore do not remember just how long we were at Newport News. But not over a few months I know.

One day we began packing up. We had orders to leave our tents standing where they were, so it did not take long to get ready. We were going to Hampton just about a mile from Fortress Monroe. I think it was about five miles or so from where we then were. I know I walked with the Regiment, although having every opportunity of riding either horseback or in a wagon.

My brother-in-law received just before he started a commission making him Major of the Regiment. He was a staff officer now and entitled to ride horseback.[11] Well we bid farewell to Newport News and arrived at Hampton the same day. And a nice place it was.

We went right into a camp already fitted up. This camp had been occupied by a New York Regiment, nearly all of whom were Germans, and members of the Turner Society.[12] They had moved out as we had, leaving their tents, etc. intact. After a very long stay here, where it seems they had been forgotten, they were now ordered to the front to do some fighting. Our Privates went into nice Sibley tents which are cone shaped as [see fig. 9] and about 12 feet high, but these tents[13] had been raised up on boards like this [see fig. 10] and were floored nicely

Fig. 9. Sibley tent sketch 1
by George Maguire.

Fig. 10. Sibley tent sketch 2
by George Maguire.

inside with every convenience. Each company had ten of these, five on each side of a broad avenue. At the head of this avenue was another broad avenue running at right angles and about 60 feet wide. Fronting this were the officer's quarters consisting of nicely built little cottages, with gardens and fences about them, and flowers in abundance. All were furnished nicely, the furniture having been taken from the houses of rebels who had gone south for fear of the Yankees. One of the officers had a nice piano. Everything was in good shape and every officer had a place. The sutler had a fine store with shelving etc. complete. But what pleased me especially was a large and well stocked gymnasium, having everything found in a first-class place of the kind in those days. The building was fully 20 feet high at the sides and built of pine trees split in half with the bark side out. It was about 60 feet by 40 with shingle roof. It was a fine gymnasium and our Regiment passed a set of resolutions of thanks which was sent the New Yorkers who left it for us, together with a big gold medal. I spent many an hour in this place, and got many a hard knock and bump and scratch and fall. Several times I remember to have crawled out, bruised and all shaken up by a fall vowing I would never go inside again, but in an hour or so I would be back again. A map of the neighborhood would show like this: [see fig. 11].

The harbor here was about five miles across. In front of our camp was the finest bathing place imaginable. One could wade out a ¼ mile before getting beyond his depth. The bottom was all a kind of packed sand with little bunches of weed growing here and there.

After the weather got warm I used to spend most of my time in

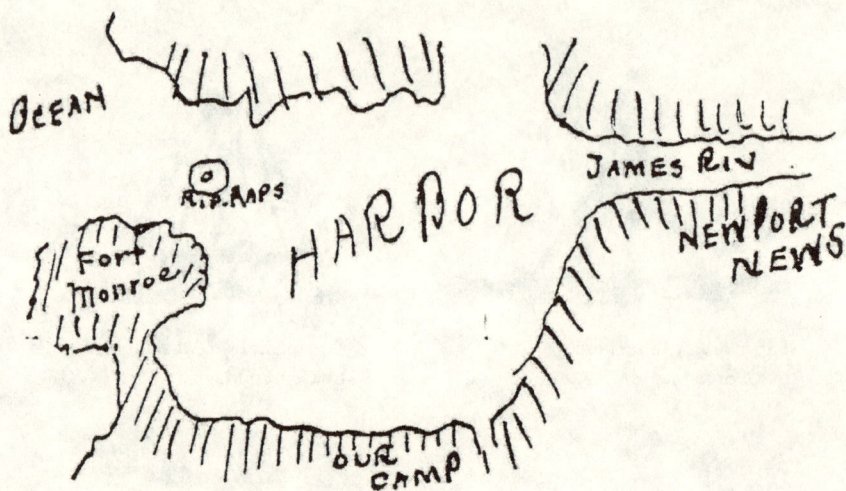

Fig. 11. Harbor sketch by George Maguire.

this water. Under these little bunches of weed that grew on the bottom I caught many a mess of crabs which I would turn over to the soldiers. Also many a mess of clams have I dug up with my toes. I was a giver of all I caught, so the men turned in and after much work they made me a small square boat or scow. I would wade around with my boat tide to me with a rope and a forked stick in my hand. I would see a crab lying low under a weed, ready to grab me by the toes should I tread on him, and pinch till the blood came, unless I could break off his claw before. Did I see him first down would go my forked stick on his back, and then I would reach down and catch him by the hind legs and throw him into the boat. Then my feet would tread on something hard and round like and I would bring up from under the sand a half or a dozen clams. Often I would fish for Black Fish and Flounders and would sometimes catch a Toad Fish. A Flounder is a queer fellow. Almost as flat as a pancake and has both his eyes on one side. The toad is a small fellow, but poke him a little and he will swell up a dozen times his size, as much as to say, "Look out! You don't know how big I am when I am mad. See that now."

Well I was in the water early and late, day after day, and week after week, until one day I came to my quarters with a chill, which was followed by the usual fever. The doctor gave me quinine in liquid form and it tasted so nasty and lasted in its bitterness so long that I could eat nothing. All I would attempt to eat would taste like quinine.

I would lie there and have fever and become delirious and think I was going out the window, floating out bed and all, and I would grab the bedding and try to keep from it and cry out for someone, but all were men. What was a sick boy? He only had chills and we had medicine right there. He was quiet in there. Better let him alone. And so I lay. Day after day until I finally got so bad that my brother-in-law thought I had better be sent to Baltimore. No! I didn't want to go home. I wanted to get well, and then said he, "I must send for "Marg." That was sister and his wife.[14] She was there in a few days and oh, how glad I was! In a short while, by having the doctor attend to me closely I was up and out and fishing again. But I did not go in the water so much myself.

Between our camp and Fortress Monroe was a very large hospital erected to receive the wounded from the Peninsular [sic].[15] One afternoon, as I passed by one of the windows in the rear, I saw them place a man on a table, then they put a strap about his legs above the knee (a tourniquet), then several men got about his leg. I was down below and could not see what they were doing, but in a short while I saw one lift up a leg which had been amputated. I was horror-struck. The awful side of war was then and there first made known to me. How awful I thought. I was so struck with the awful sight that I hardly knew what

Fig. 12. Chesapeake Hospital, Hampton, Va., Dec. 1864. Library of Congress.

to do. I finally started on a run for my tent, and falling into my sister's lap I cried for an hour before I could tell them what it was about. I got so worked up that they had to have the doctor come to give me something to quiet me. For days and days I would not go near this hospital but I got over it in a moment and inside of five minutes, from being so fearful of such things. I became as it were immured to them, so I could go anywhere about a wounded person without any feeling, only pity and sorrow for their suffering. [See fig. 12.]

One day, coming up past the hospital I saw a lot of flat cars had arrived. No cars were ever there before, but it appears, the road that had been torn up was fixed up in some way, enough to permit these old, rickety and patched up flat cars, loaded with wounded soldiers, with wounds days old, stinking so loud one could hardly go near the cars, to be brought in. I was gazing on with my old feeling of horror, when a man (a surgeon I afterwards learned) said, "Here Bub! Make yourself useful.[16] Take this bucket of water and give these men until we get them off." I changed at once. I thought this was orders from the head of the War Dept. itself and I dare not refuse. I believe had I known he had no authority over me I would have taken to my heels. But I was ever after glad of my ignorance at the time. I took the water in that bucket and about fifty more and I gave water to this man until I thought he would surely burst himself. "Pour a little on here please?" "Oh! Thanks was ever a thing so grateful." "This way son, I'm dying with thirst." "God be thankful for pure water." "We have come a long way and have suffered much, but the pleasure from that drink seems worth it all." And hearing such remarks I forgot fear, and smell and stink, and when I was through watering, I remained until dark doing what I could for any and every one. "Your awful handy," said the surgeon "hand me that bottle." "Thread this needle for me please? My eyes can't see the eye as quick as yours." And so I saw wounds dressed, cuts made, and an arm amputated that afternoon, but had no fear and afterwards I was at the hospital when a man was dead here, another just dying over there, one yelling with delirium in that cot, a young fellow crying out with pain, because the surgeon hurt him, yet they could not give him an anesthetic for some reason, and in the operating room a leg was being taken amputated, but I never had the feeling experienced when I saw that first operation.

It was not very long before "The Army of the Peninsula" as it was called, began its return, not having been successful.[17] All the way was swamps, lagoons, etc., and there were more men sick than well, and so they returned, embarking in the transports at Fortress Monroe.[18] With our regiment was a young Negro chap who had not very much to do, or if he had, he did not do it. While watching the army embarking, an officer rode up to him on the wharf and asked if he wanted a horse! Answering in the affirmative, he gave him the horse he was riding, with saddle, bridle and all. Government vessels would not carry horses for any officers but those entitled to ride in the infantry. Only officers from Major up could take their horses on board. Consequently this officer, who was a Captain, had to leave his horse. He was a tolerable good animal, nothing extra. Well John—the negro—rode him into camp and brought him to me. He knew that he would not be allowed to keep a horse, and so he invested me with a half interest, or made me an equal partner. John had a kind of shed built up against our house, big enough to allow him to have his bunk across it. There was no window in this shed, but there was a V-shaped hole cut in the door. I took the horse to try and John went off to the fort. When I returned, it struck me that we must have a shelter for our animal, a stable. I finally thought of John's shed so I put him in there. It was wide enough, but it crowded him for length. The door could only be closed by pulling his tail through the notch in the door, and it was not long before a tail attracted a crowd of jokers who found lots of fun at my expense. John slept on a husk mattress which the horse must have thought was good provender, as he made very short work of the middle of it. John wasn't satisfied to have his lodgings made into a horse stable so we built a shelter for him over against the far side of the gymnasium.[19] About a ½ mile from our camp was a lot of government stables, large enough for probably 1000 horses. Horses had been kept here for replenishing the army that had been up on the Peninsular. All had been taken away but about 150 and many of these were sick. A big trench had been dug some distance away when a horse was discovered to have glanders or any hurt or disease that made them worthless, they would be taken out to this trench, stood up beside it, and shot in the head. A push would send them into the trench and they would be covered deep with dirt. At these stables I got my feed for my horse and lots of it.

I was personally acquainted with most of the soldiers and officers of our regiment and all of them were ready for a joke at any time. They would get my horse and hide him between the tents, or take him inside often. I would hunt all over and finally some soldier would come leading him up as if they had just caught him running wild. I treated

this horse well myself and he was beginning to look up, but my partner took a notion that he would like to ride, which was all right. But
every time he would have him out, the horse would appear exhausted
for a day or two afterward. Soon I began to hear of his hard riding and
ill-treatment of the poor old horse. So I told him if he didn't do better
when he had the horse out I would give him away. Not long after the
Negros had a pow-wow, and he rode out to it. When he returned, I determined he should never have an opportunity of treating this horse
so badly again. From early morning until late at night the saddle had
never been off. The horse had had nothing to eat and little to drink.
Other Negros had ridden him and raced him, and he was nearly dead.
So next morning I gave him to the foreman of the government stables, and that was the last of my partnership in horse flesh.

There was a peculiar fish or crustaceous fish to be found on the
beach here. One would see little holes in the sand after the tide went
out and as you stepped near them, little streams of water would spurt
up about a foot high. By digging down about a foot or a little over you
would find a sort of clam, shaped the same almost as a clam, only the
shell was longer and dark, almost black. A small protuberance about a
quarter inch long stuck out between the shells, and this would be extended from where they laid to the surface, and from this they would
spurt the water as you passed by them.

The village of Hampton was probably about a quarter mile from
our camp.[20] I used to visit it occasionally. We had a walk of perhaps a
quarter mile (maybe more or less) and come to a creek, called Hampton Creek, which was spanned by a bridge about 200 feet wide. On
the near side of this bridge was a large house occupied by a family of
Octoroons, the whitest and fairest of all people having Negro blood in
their veins.[21] The bridge crossing Hampton Creek had been completely
destroyed by the rebels and our army had re-built it or built a new one.
It was not a very solid affair, for one day as a lot of cattle were being
driven over, the bridge sank until the floor in two places reached the
water almost and was very difficult to get a team over it. The bridge
looked like this: [see fig. 13] and a funny looking affair it was. At one
time the rebels thought they could capture Fortress Monroe and they
tried it, but had to give it up. They burnt Hampton Creek Bridge and
remained in Hampton Village which was all rebel inhabitants. In order
to get them out, our army had to shell them, and in this way Hampton
Village was destroyed. My first visit to Hampton was on a Sabbath day.
There was not one house standing in the place. There was a wall here,
and a big chimney place over there, but nothing complete. The ruin

Fig. 13. Bridge sketch by George Maguire.

was also complete [sic]. I found a cannon ball occasionally, unexploded shell, and a can of small iron balls the size of a medium small apple (these were called grape and canister or grapeshot in canister).[22] Fences were still about a great number of yards, filled with beautiful flowers. Fruit trees were plentiful, broken furniture was everywhere but no living soul occupied what was not long before this a most beautiful little place. I guess the people thought the "Yanks" would certainly show them "no quarter" as they all fled south. [See fig. 14.]

What a lazy, careless, and indifferent but enjoyable life these people of Hampton had lived. A very little work during the year brought them enough for groceries and clothing. Fashion not being closely followed down there, one good suit or dress would last many years.

Fig. 14. Ruins of Hampton Church, Va., west end. The oldest church in America. July 2, 1862. George N. Barnard (1819–1902), photographer. Library of Congress.

Fig. 15. Well with buckets sketch
by George Maguire.

Vegetables grew in abundance by simply planting and keeping out the weeds. Fine fruit was everywhere and apples of the finest quality. Fish and clams had only to be gone after. Truly, here was a second paradise, but I should not wonder but that many of them after talked of going out into the world, to a better country and climate. Where would they find it?

Our soldiers had been left every convenience by that New York Regiment.[23] A splendid place for cooking. I might say a regular kitchen. They had dug a well for each company and sunk barrels for bracing. Then a high post stood up with a long reach over it like this: [see fig. 15] which made it easy to draw water. Everything was so nice and convenient that our regiment would have been well pleased to have remained right here until the war was over, but rumors became rife that the rebels were moving down through Maryland "on to Washington" and Baltimore and the Maryland Regiments would be needed to protect their own state and cities. After a while orders came to move to Fort Monroe and take a steamer for Washington. It was hard for many to leave such pleasant surroundings and comfortable quarters, but all seemed anxious for a change, and they got it.[24]

CHAPTER 3

INTO BATTLE AT
ANTIETAM

One day in September we marched down to the wharf and went aboard the steamer. It did not take long to get all aboard and then we steamed away from "Old Point Comfort" some of us never to see the ocean again and me, in particular, never to so thoroughly enjoy a summer. We followed up the beautiful Potomac and on the way a kind of stiff felt hat was given out to the whole regiment. Soon after I began seeing them floating in the wake of the steamer. From a few disposing of these serviceable and becoming hats in this way, it soon became a panic or mania and nearly 900 hats were floating down the Potomac. Those who wished to wear them were prevented, as they were snatched from their heads and overboard they went. Many wished they had such a hat after getting on the road and in the hot sun. Those few who saved theirs by hiding them away were the envy of the other hot-headed and foolish fellows.

We arrived in Washington the next day and laid about for an hour or two.[1] It was perhaps 3:00 p.m. when we arrived. No one was permitted to leave the regiment to go anywhere and we could only see the city from the wharf. About 5:00 p.m. the order was given to fall in. I had a fine knapsack and in it lots of things I wished to preserve; relics, curiosities, etc., besides stamps and a suit of clothing that had never yet been worn, as well as a new pair of shoes my sister had just sent me. When we started I threw the knapsack on one of our wagons and from that time to this I have never seen it. The many thieves around and about Washington did not permit anything to escape their voracious maws or clutches. We marched about two miles outside the city and halted in the middle of an open field and camped. We had no tents of any kind, and we soon felt we had left a very soft berth at

Old Point Comfort. It was a cool afternoon and cloudy and soon after camping it began to drizzle—a September drizzle—We made a pot of coffee and having some hard tack we made our supper. About dark it began a slow and steady rain, which lasted all night. We had a big fire of fence rails, but we could only warm and dry one side while the other was getting wet. My brother-in-law (who shall be known here after as Salome Marsh) and a Lieutenant laid their blankets down on the grass. I got between them, and with a rubber blanket on top we retired. I slept for a while, but was awakened by a soft stream of water running down my neck. Of course I had to get up and dry out, which I did by sitting beside the fire the balance of the night. Lying between two men made what was a kind of valley where the water gathered and when someone moved it sent the water forward and down my neck. It was a most unpleasant experience, so much so, that I have never forgotten that night.

I sat up most of the night and it was certainly a most uncomfortable one. In the morning we made a pot of coffee and with our hard tack got our breakfast. About 8 a.m. the bugle sounded and we were again on the march. On leaving camp at Hampton every soldier packed up a big pile of luggage and many of them had as much as a mule ought to carry. They had collected little things around them which they hated to leave and so they tried to carry them along. After marching a half day the sun came out then and it was warm. Men soon saw they could not keep up and carry all they had with them, so they began ridding themselves of superfluous luggage and for miles and miles the sides of the roads were covered with all kinds of stuff that could be carried no further. Blankets, overcoats and clothing of every description, in fact a little of everything seemed to be strewn along the road. I have since often thought how well the farmers must have fared were they in need of any of the stuff left along the edges of their farms. Books and papers were plentiful and many fine works could be seen tossed to one side.

Paper currency had been issued but a short time and I had some of it with me. At one little town an old lady was out her back gate offering some most delicious looking pies for sale. I wanted one ever so much but couldn't get it, the old lady refusing my 50¢ note. I tried to persuade her, but to no purpose, and I had to do without. Day after day we marched along. I trod every foot. There was a steady stream of soldier, wagons, artillery, cavalry and ambulances as far along the road as one could see, the dust at times was terrible, but I didn't mind it. The road was full of stragglers and every now and then some poor fellow that from sickness or some other cause could go no further afoot. Along came the rear guard with its surgeons and the way-siders were examined. If sick or disabled they were put into wagons or ambulances. If they were shirkers, they were forced to get up and "hoof" it with the rest.[2]

We reached Monocacy Junction finally the cars turned off here and crossing the Monocacy River on a very high bridge went on to Frederick[3] which was distant about five miles. This big bridge had been destroyed by the rebels who were ahead of us-how far we knew not-and whom we were trying to come up with or overtake.[4] Our Engineers had built another bridge which was below this on which we crossed. As I passed over this bridge my attention was called to a man laying under the destroyed railroad bridge away down on the rocks below, "A dead rebel" someone said, "must have fallen off while helping to burn the bridge." It was a sad sight to me and as young as I was I thought that some family away down south was even then wondering just where he was, what he was doing and perhaps praying for his safety.

We passed through Frederick (the home of Barbara Fritchie) with bugles blowing and drums beating and amid much cheering.[5] We didn't stop, only long enough to get water to drink and fill our canteens, but pushed right on. We heard the rebel army was just ahead, having passed through Frederick only a few days before. I was quite tired when we reached the next little town (the name of which I forget) and here we stopped awhile.

My brother-in-law knowing it would not be many days before we would have a battle persuaded me to turn back home. We went to the hotel and put me in the charge of the proprietor to be taken by team back to Monocacy and from there I was to take the cars for home.[6] He bade me good-bye as the bugle sounded for the march and left me. I remained about five minutes at the hotel. My brother-in-law tells it this way. "I was glad to have George with me and although he was company yet he was a constant worry for fear something would happen him or he would get sick. I had studied for days how I was to get him turned towards home. His mother and sisters were worrying themselves sick about him and when I had left him at [the hotel] and made all the arrangements so that he would get home safely. I felt relieved of a heavy worry yet I was very sorry to lose him. I had been marching along leading my horse for about twenty minutes and was talking to an officer. I was telling him about leaving George behind (everyone knew George in our regiment) and I noticed that he looked amused, but I kept on, told him how it would save me much worry etc. Nearly all the regiment already knew that I had left him, and when I had gotten through with telling this officer about it he remarked 'who is that behind there? I looked back and there trudging along behind the horse was George. Such a howl of laughter went up from those who knew the circumstance never was heard before in that regiment. George only smiled and I had to smile too. I tried to get George to take turns with me riding my horse, but when he saw a big blister on my foot which I was trying to open, nothing could persuade him to take another turn. My horse was big and powerful enough to carry us both, but he wouldn't ride anymore and nearly the whole ninety miles to Antietam and thirty five back to Monocacy he walked."

After I was left at the hotel I felt sorry I had allowed myself to be left behind and without thinking of anyone but myself I put out after my brother-in-law. We had much trouble to get enough water fit to drink on this march. I have waited at a spring where the water had been dipped dry for more to run in and had then to take half sand or mud to get a little. I have drunk water that a horse would turn away from in disgust. At times on this march it was difficult to get even hard-tack and salt pork, and many a meal consisted of green apples and common corn from the field roasted in the fire.

I remember camping one evening near a potato patch and the owner stood guard with a shot gun. One of the officers offered him an order on the government for his pay. "Damn the Government," said the fool, which was no sooner out of his mouth than Biff, the officer, took him under the jaw and down he went. The officer grabbed the gun and raised it to hit the fellow, when another officer caught it and no doubt saved the farmers life. The consequence was that the farmer sneaked away to his horse and by morning there was not a potato in his patch and he got no order for pay for them either.[7]

The morning after I had been left at the hotel we were on the march earlier than usual. We had been camped some distance from the road and in getting back to it we crossed over the foot of South Mountain. A small battle or heavy skirmish fight had been fought here the day before and the ground showed it to have been a fierce fight.[8] The dead were being buried and the wounded carried back to better places. Here and there lay a poor fellow waiting his turn to be put in his final resting place. Everything belonging to an army was scattered broadcast over this field at the foot of South Mountain. It was a gruesome sight in the early morning and it would be hard to say what the thoughts of the soldiers who passed over this field were, it being their first view of the aftermath of a battle. It produced its effect on me I know. Passing over this field we came into the road again. About fifty yards ahead was a big tree at one side of the road. In the early morning light I could see there was a person leaning against it, having as I thought sat down to rest. I wondered that anyone would be resting so early in the day, but I found it was even so. A Confederate soldier was taking his last rest. He had broken his musket in half before stretching himself out to die. Where he was wounded we could not tell by looking and so we conjectured that finding he had a fatal wound he braced himself to reach the shade of this tree. With his last strength he clubbed his musket and brought it down against the tree trunk with sufficient force to break it in half at the stock. The jar must have caused a fresh flow of blood from his wound, but the gun would be useless to any of the two armies as would he. He put his back against the tree as he sat down and began thinking of home (what thoughts). He grew weaker and weaker during the night. "Oh for a little water," he may have cried. In the first hours of the morning he must have died. We passed on and he was soon forgotten. I have noticed this one man, as he was the only one I saw either dead or wounded, away from the battle field.

We marched all day. Stopping but a short while at noon for rest and about 3:00 p.m. we began to hear the boom of big guns. Troop after troop of Cavalry went rushing by. Artillery had to be given the road every little while, the ambulances by the hundreds, six-mule wagons loaded with hard tack, salt, pork, beans etc., etc., and caissons filled with ammunition. All this passing caused a horrible dust, which with no water to drink caused a choking up that was hard to stand. We struggled on until 6:00 p.m. when we came to a stream of water clear and bright. It was too cold for a plunge, but all washed as well as they could that wanted to and we had all the water we could drink. Our bed was as usual sheltered by a few boughs slanted against a tree, under which we placed out blankets. All night we could hear the boom of cannon, and knew that ere-long some who were here with us, would be among the dead, wounded or missing. A young fellow named Price called me one evening up to where he had his knapsack and showing me several packages of letters (from his sweetheart I surmised) asked me, if possible should he be killed in battle, would I try to find him and his knapsack and destroy these letters. He was killed at the battle of Antietam as he was getting over a fence. I could not destroy his letters. Had I been a man I would have hunted him out but being a boy I had no thought at the time for anything. It was just as well I guess, as hardly anyone cares to read another's letters, and in case they do, they know not the parties who wrote them nor to whom they were written. We were up early in the morning and on the march again. The roads were so full of teams that our regiment could move but slowly. It was a struggle.

At nearly dusk this evening we came to Antietam bridge—a big stone culvert that crossed the road.[9] [See fig. 16.] We were tired out, dusty and awful hungry yet we could get nothing to eat but hard tack. We could not make a fire to boil our coffee as we were within the range of the Confederate sharp-shooters so, after munching some crackers and drinking a lot of water, my brother found some fence post, put them up against a stone wall and putting our blankets in and under, on the ground, we crawled in and went to bed. All night again, the boom of cannon kept up, and as we were close enough to hear the whizz of shell and solid shot as it passed over us, and could feel the jar as the balls struck the ground. We did not sleep without some anxiety. We were secure enough, but we had two brothers and many friends who were unprotected and we thought of them whenever we were awake, which was quite often.

It was the "night before the battle" many thought, and their fate would be known before another sleep. But not so.[10] In the morning we

Fig. 16. Antietam Bridge, Maryland, September 1862, printed later, ca. 1866. Alexander Gardner (1821–1882), photographer. Library of Congress.

were up early and cooked our pot of coffee and ate our hard tack. Our regiment had its arms all stacked and the men were straggling about, some resting under the trees, a few of which were around. Instead of having rail fences in this part of Maryland, many of the farmers were separated by stone walls. Stones that were picked off the land were used for this purpose. All day long a fierce battle between the artillery was kept up, and every once in a while a shell or cannon ball would reach us and then there would be a scampering for fear it was a shell and was going to burst. I remember that one of our officers was sitting on a barrel of beans, when a shot struck the barrel near the ground, let out the beans or part of them, but as luck would have it no one was injured. I kept close to my brother-in-law, and we went back on the side of a hill to get a view, if possible, of the battle. We had a colored servant who we lost in Washington and we found him again only the night before. He was terribly frightened when he heard the cannon and the shell and shot whizzing in the air. When we started up on the side of the hill, he said he would go up "dar behind dat stone wall." He started for that wall, about a 100 yards distant and we have never seen him since. Guess he started back to Washington or Baltimore. Nothing of consequence occurred during the balance of the day and night, although the firing of the artillery was constant all the time.

The next morning we were up early, orders were given to be in a hurry and after eating a mouthful the Regiment fell into line and we marched. "Going into battle" was the word.[11] My brother-in-law said, "George you keep with Dr. Norris," (that was the chief surgeon of our regiment and a friend and neighbor of ours in Baltimore) and he told the Dr. to keep an eye on me that I didn't get away.[12] "You stay close by me George and take this case of instruments," so I followed. Instead of crossing Antietam Creek on the bridge, we marched across the road and after going about 100 yards down its bank we forded it, by wading in water nearly to the waist.[13] On the opposite side was a corn field and so many men had gone over and dripped the water from their clothing on to this soft ground that it had become a sea of mud that was hard to pull ourselves through.[14]

The Regiment was marching four abreast. They marched in this order up alongside a fence on the left, on the other side of which was a body of timber. When they all gotten up, still marching alongside this fence, the order was given, "left flank!" That means that the regiment should turn half way around (each man) to the left, and keep right on. As the regiment made this movement it faced the fence. It seemed

to me that every man's hand caught that fence at the same moment
and down it came. We could hear the rattle of musketry not far away,
and our men though when they "left flanked" into this timber and
wheeled to the right on a "double quick march" they were right onto
the enemy. Such a yelling, as they started off on a run. Haversacks
and knapsacks, in fact everything almost except gun, ammunition
and sword was left in this timber, never to be seen again. I followed
behind, stopping long enough to snatch a handful of sugar from an
open haversack that some poor fellow had left. The enemy was not in
this timber; on we rushed through and out of it across a field in the
middle of which was a little stream of water. And here was where I got
lost from our regiment.[15]

Water was what I wanted, and I believe, had the whole army been
fighting at me I would have gotten my canteen filled. Our regiment
was going on a run when they crossed this little stream.[16] It was only
about a foot from bank to bank, dirty and black by the many feet that
had accidentally trod into it. I stopped and scooped out a hole in the
mud and put my canteen in to fill it. While doing this, another regiment passed over me and I was cut off from ours. I didn't seem to care.
I knew it was ahead there somewhere, and when my canteen was filled
on I went again straight ahead, right into the midst of the battle. The
balls were hitting everywhere "spit, spat, whiz" they would go singing
a long drawn out "ping" as they passed on. "Whir-r-r" a shell was going
overhead. It had passed when we heard the sound, but we dodged it
just the same, then a cannon ball would go whizzing overhead and
another dodge. The din was awful. We were in a corn field that had
been planted in an orchard. I got behind an apple tree and wondered
what I should do. I still held the case of instruments under my arm
and was wishing the doctor had them wherever he was. The wounded
were being assisted or carried past me. I was peering from behind the
tree when I heard my name shouted. Turning about I saw one of our
surgeons who looked frightened. He beckoned and I ran to him. "We
have been looking for you everywhere and Dr. Norris is almost wild,
come on quick." I followed him back about 100 yards to a big barn.[17] A
large red blanket had been run up on a pole to denote a hospital and as
much as possible keep either side from firing in that direction.[18] As I
handed over the instruments, the doctor gave me a bunch of canteens
to get full of water. I started down to the spring house about twenty
five yards distant and looking inside I found the floor covered with
crocks full of milk. I filled up on milk as I was awful hungry and no

prospect of food. A nice little stream was running down here and after I drank all the milk I wanted I stepped outside to fill the canteens. Almost fifty feet from where I was I noticed a bugler get down flat on his stomach to take a drink. I was about to call him to come and get some milk, but the noise was such that I thought he would not hear me, so I held my tongue. I have often thought since that if I had called I might have saved his life. I began filling my canteens and had one or two filled when a shell burst, as it seemed, directly over my head in the air above. I heard some parts of it sound "spat" as it struck the ground. It scared me for a moment but I kept at my work. Soon I noticed in the water, a slight color and a thread of red that looked like blood. I stood up to see where it might come from and there was the bugler, in the same position, as if drinking, but his head was mashed into the sand and water, the brain was spattered around and the little stream was being discolored by it. He was dead. A piece of the shell that had bursted over his head had killed him. I took my canteens and got up to the hospital in quick time reporting the reason for not filling all them.

I remained at the hospital until afternoon. The first man brought in was an officer. One man was assisting him on each sidearm, and I thought to myself here is a desperately wounded man, but when I saw his wounds it made me smile. A musket ball had grazed his forehead cutting the skin and probably giving him a hard knock against his cranium. He wasn't hurt a bit. He might have imagined he was shot through the head and would no doubt be dead in a short while. I think he was a little ashamed after being examined to know how little he was injured. Here were three men taken from the fight for no cause.

Shell and solid shot were coming over our way thicker than ever, so I went up out of the fence that made a small enclosure around the barn to get behind a big straw stack that was just outside the fence. While standing there a soldier and quite an old man came up. He was bent way over forward and with both hands on his "bread basket." "What's the matter," said I. "Shot in the stomach," he answered. "I see no blood, let's see where you are hurt?" Reaching into his shirt bosom he felt around and pulled his hand out, he exhibited a musket ball. He seemed overjoyed that the ball had not entered his stomach, but he did not go back to try it again.

The orderly Sergeant of one of the Companies of our regiment was a very large man named Eager. I knew him well. I saw him being assisted in by two men and I hurried to him to find out how badly he had been wounded. I inquired where he was wounded and one of the men replied, "He's not wounded, he's sick." I told the doctor and he answered, "his backbone wants a little stiffening." Thinking that was something that was necessary to be done I went back to them and said to the men "stiffen his backbone, that will cure him. The Doctor says so." The men smiled, but the Sergeant only groaned and lay down on a soft bunch of straw.

The wounded began gathering thick in an hour or so after the Doctors were ready. They were lying around the barnyard every available space being taken up. The Doctor's had their hands full and leg after leg and arm after arm was amputated with a recklessness that was astounding. Many amputations were no doubt wholly unnecessary but this was war.[19] Quite a little pile of limbs were lying about the rude table the Surgeons had rigged up. I gathered them up into one heap out of the way and helped at what I could until I began feeling sick. From being hungry I guess. I hadn't thought of eating, but my stomach had, and so I started away from the hospital towards the rear. The fighting was still going on as rigorous as ever. Just as I got outside the barnyard a shell or shot struck a big tree about ten yards in front of me and down came a big limb it had torn off. A little way further on I met a lady who had just alighted from an ambulance. She had on what looked like a man's coat, a short grey skirt and what looked to be a pair of men's pants under the skirt. She asked me whose boy I was, where I was from, etc., and then passed on to the hospital. I afterward heard she was Miss Clara Barton, and equal to a half dozen Surgeons among the wounded.[20]

I kept on to the rear and when about 150 yards from the hospital I saw a young fellow lying beside the road with his head on a stone. He was wounded terribly. A cannon ball had cut through his shoulder and left his arm hanging by a few ligaments. I was close enough to see the quivering of the lacerated flesh. I didn't go to him, nor try to do anything for him. Not even to ask if he would like a drink of water. One thing, I had no water with me, my canteen having been left for use at the Hospital. I have, hundreds of times yes, thousands of times since, wished I had done what I could for him, had gone to him and spoke a few kind words at least. I can only account for my not doing so by my age and inexperience and thoughtlessness. Like the priest in the parable, I "passed by on the other side." I met many parties more or less wounded back here in the rear. Two men were carrying an officer in a rubber blanket. He had been hit in one temple by a musket ball and it had passed clear through his head, forcing his eyes out on his cheeks. He was only breathing and could live only a short while. I told the men so. But they said they would get him to the hospital and try and have something done for him. "We'll do all we can for him, he is from our country and home, and we could never look his people in the face if we ever get back there if we didn't," and they lifted their friend and went in the direction of the hospital which I had pointed out to them. How these men, so many of them passed by the hospital I couldn't understand. Probably they didn't know what the big red flag (blanket) was an emblem of, on an occasion of this kind.

I began thinking of my two brothers who were taking part in the battle, whether they would escape, where they were at this time and what doing. William or "Bill" as we named, was careful and I knew would look out for himself, but "Joe" the elder of the two was careless, rash and brave, and for him I felt anxious. I was certain he would do some fool-hardy thing and I had a strong inkling (some would say premonition) knowing his recklessness, that he would not escape a wound. Everyone liked him, and he knew it, and I sometimes thought he'd done those reckless performances to gain favor.[21]

I kept on my sauntering to the rear until I found myself beside a bunch of Confederate soldiers who had been captured. I was examining them from a distance of ten or twelve feet, when the order was given to move them to some other locality. I was dumbfounded when I was ordered to fall in with them and I suppose I would have been compelled to go, had I not been able to prove who I was. I was dressed in a suit of what was called "Confederate Grey" a color and material that was the prevailing style in Baltimore and this had given the parties in charge the idea that I was a "rebel." I kept from too near prisoners after that. It was getting well on towards evening. I saw quite a group of officers and on a hill just beyond and I went to where they was, and found myself close to General McClellan and staff.[22] I had a good look at them and them at me. Just then an officer came galloping up at full speed and spoke to the General and handed him a piece of paper. The General read and spoke to the officer and gave his arm a sweeping motion as if he would gather in the large number of stragglers who were everywhere about seeming to have deserted their comrades in battle and come to the rear to keep out of danger. The officer turned and with a number more of the General's staff began gathering up the stragglers. "Fall in every one of you," and those that didn't fall in in a hurry were forced. I had to fall in too, but what I was to do I didn't have the slightest idea. We marched off but hadn't gone over a 100 yards when another officer came riding up and shouted, "We have taken it, they are routed, it is ours," and we were disbanded (we stragglers) at once. I found out that there had been a fierce struggle all day for possession of a stone bridge over Antietam Creek. First one side would have it and then the other. We were losing ground when the officer first rode up to General McClellan for reinforcements. The reserves were there, but he wouldn't send them, but told his officers to gather in these stragglers and in case they failed he would send the "reserves." I was saved a battle on a bridge.[23]

It was getting dark. I had become lost for sure. I hardly knew which way to go or where. I did not know north from south. I didn't seem to care much about being lost but I was awful hungry. I hadn't had a mouthful to eat since early morning. Away over to my left I saw a party sitting around a fire. I hurried over and found they were being furnished with "rations." I got in between two of them and got a chuck of fat pork and some crackers. I found a stick and putting my piece of pork on the end of it was holding it over the fire. It was quite dark by this time, all musketry fire had ceased, but the artillery was still shelling the confederates. I was holding my meat over the fire and wondering where I was to sleep when someone said "Well this is fortunate! Here you are. Why your brother has five hundred men looking for you." I looked up and there was Dr. Norris our Surgeon. I was well pleased. "Come on," he said and away we went. It was dark as pitch. Every once in a while we would stumble over a man. Dead I know, and I would shudder. But I finally reached our camp. They were all glad to see me and I to see them. I found my brother-in-law unhurt although a ball had passed through his coat. My brother "Bill" had been skimmed by a ball ploughing along his arm, taking only the skin for about eight inches and leaving a red mark which was sore for quite a while afterwards but Joe was wounded. As usual he had been too brave. "He ran clear up to the rebel entrenchments and fired right down among them" they all said. A foolhardy action. He was shot in the leg, the ball splintering the bone. He was taken to another hospital, his wound dressed and then put into an ambulance and the next we heard of him he was in Philadelphia in a hospital there.[24]

We found our sutler had arrived with his wagon, and we had cheese and cookies, etc., for supper instead of salt pork.

After supper we talked about my going home. I wanted to go now. I had had a rough time and was satisfied now to go home to Baltimore. My brother-in-law didn't know where they would be ordered to next and how many battles they might have to fight and at any time something might happen to me. Two wounded men would start for Baltimore in the morning. They would walk to Monocacy Junction (35 miles) and take the train from there for Baltimore. In the morning we said good bye and started on our long walk. I had a blanket rolled up and carried over my shoulder. The two men, being wounded, could carry very little. Both had bad wounds. One shot in the arm and the other through the shoulder. We had enough to eat for one day. At night we crawled under a hay stack. I slept between them, but I never again want to sleep with a wounded person. An old wound has a peculiar smell. It does not smell as would any decaying animal but more like the smell we notice from a dead person. It is sickening.

We ran out of food the next day. One of the boys went to a farm house to beg something. He got a slab of bread and butter and brought it to us intact to divide, but I could not take a part. Both seemed so weak and so much in need of food, that ravenously hungry as I was, I could not have eaten it from them. I ate corn and green apples until we got to Frederick where-having some money—I purchased a square meal for the three of us.

We arrived at Monocacy at nearly dark and there was a train just about to leave. We got aboard. I was so tired out that I went to sleep and awoke long enough to settle my fare and then slept until I reached Baltimore. I took a street car, and when it was known on the car that I had just come from Antietam, I was surrounded by people wanting to hear the news. All the Maryland regiments were in this battle and as most of them were from Baltimore, everyone seemed to have a friend in the fight they were anxious to hear from. Of course I could tell them but little. I answered questions until I was tired out. I was so dead tired, so utterly exhausted that while I was being plied with questions on the car I fell back in a dead faint. I soon revived and heard them saying, "The poor boy is nearly dead." "Should have had a hack," but I finally got off the car near home. It was dark and I walked the four blocks to my home. Our house had a vacant lot on the side through which we always entered, going to the back or dining room door. As I entered and passed the window I saw my mother lying on the lounge with her face buried in a pillow weeping. She had three sons and a son in law in the battle of Antietam (counting myself whom she thought being present must have caused me to be in it) and she had heard no word from either. The papers had stated that our Regiment (the 5th

Maryland) had suffered severely in killed and wounded, but could give no names for a few days.[25] Of course I was hugged and kissed and made much of. I brought the first authentic news from the battle and it was not so bad for our family. A neighbor happened in and almost immediately left to spread the news that George Maguire is home from the war. In a short while our house was crowded inside and out to hear from friends. I could give news to but a few regarding their friends as I had left the field before it was known the number killed and wounded. I was so tired that they put me to bed. I would sleep only on the floor. I remember that all night long I was dreaming of troops of soldiers marching into battle, drums beating and cannons firing and I awoke in the morning right glad that I was home once more. Before I was hardly through breakfast the people began calling, droves of them, in wagons, carriages and hacks, a steady stream and it kept me busy answering questions. I was glad that I could say in many cases, "Oh! He wasn't hurt. I saw him after the battle all right and well." A number had to be told of their friends being killed or wounded, among whom was the sister of the young man who had asked me that in case he was killed would I destroy the letters in his knapsack. He was one of the first to be shot, a ball passing through his head as he was getting over a fence. Death was instantaneous they said but as for his letters, I have before stated that it was impossible for me to get them as I left early the next morning after the battle. People came from every part of the city having seen by the papers I had got home.

I was a hero for a few days, but after a while we settled down and in a few weeks I was started to school again. I was so gapped at by everyone that it became a bore to me and it was worse at school. I had been out of school so long it was like a prison to be cooped up again. It worried me and I became sick. I remained away from school for quite a while. All the time I was anxious to get back with my brother-in-law. The Regiment was at Harpers Ferry, VA.[26] Finally just before Christmas my brother-in-law sent for me to come to Harpers Ferry. I got ready and just a couple of days before Christmas I started. Everybody in Baltimore seemed to be preparing for celebrating Christmas when I was on my way to a desolate place. I didn't care so much about going as I thought I would, but I went.

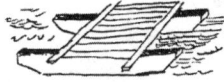

CHAPTER 4

UNION OCCUPATION
OF HARPERS FERRY,
1862–1863

My brother-in-law and another officer was at the cars to meet me on arrival and having secured my traps we started over one of the worst roads I ever saw to an Island in the Shenandoah River about a mile beyond Harpers Ferry, where the Regiment was encamped. Harpers Ferry is at the junction of the Potomac and the Shenandoah Rivers and is hemmed in on all sides by mountains.[1] The place itself had but two streets, one on a level and running through the place and on to and past the island where we had our tents and the other street ran up the side of Bolivar Heights almost steep enough to fall out of. My brother-in-law was Provost Marshall of the City (a kind of military Governor) and I spent my time between his office, the camp, and in wandering about Harpers Ferry. The U.S. had a big arsenal there at one time, where arms of all kinds were made for use of its army, but the rebels had burned it and it was in ruins. The little old engine house in which John Brown fortified himself was still standing.[2] It was a one story small concern and was pointed out to everyone who choose to make inquiry about him whose "soul goes marching on." I have ridden horse back up the Maryland Heights where the road was so steep we had to lie down on our stomachs and hold on to the horses mane to keep from sliding off. I visited every part of Harpers Ferry and explored every place I could get into.

Jefferson Rock, a big stone weighing hundreds of tons and seemingly liable to tumble over at any moment was a formidable place to me. A little stream ran down the mountain side near it and here I use to set my water wheels. I had much to amuse me but no company and so I had to go it alone. There had been two big bridges leading out of

Fig. 17. Pontoon bridge sketch by George Maguire.

Harpers Ferry. One a railroad bridge of the Baltimore & Ohio Railroad across the Potomac and the other a wagon bridge crossing the Shenandoah to Loudoun Heights in Virginia. Both had been destroyed by the Confederates, only the big stone piers remaining. Our army had a pontoon bridge across the Potomac, which answered every purpose, except for railroad cars to cross. A pontoon bridge is built of boats or pontoons and looks like the following: [see fig. 17] The pontoons are about five feet wide and very stout. Both the Potomac and Shenandoah Rivers were unnavigable here, full of big rocks that poked themselves high above the water, but just far enough between to prevent crossing

Fig. 18. Jones' Landing, Virginia (vicinity). Pontoon bridge across the James River, ca. 1861–1869. Library of Congress.

on foot except by having a foot bridge here and there. Both rivers are terrible when the water is high. [See fig. 18 and fig. 19.]

I was looking around our tent one morning when my attention was drawn to a big revolver that was left by someone. It was loaded and now thought I, I will see how well I can shoot. I went out, put up a mark and went back to fire, the hammer being hard to lift I was push-ing on it when the revolver went off, the ball passing between my fin-gers and leaving them stinging with powder. I was certain I had been shot, but when I found out I was not, I then and there declared I would never again meddle with a fire arm without I had occasion to use it and I never have.

Harpers Ferry was an awful muddy hole. We remained there all winter and early in the spring we got orders to break camp and take the cars for Point of Rocks.[3] This was a little place of five or six houses, a few store buildings, all empty, one hotel and a depot. My brother-in-law was appointed Provost Marshall under Fish[4] of Baltimore City who was chief Provost of all points on the Potomac River where persons could cross from north to south and vice versa. I was made clerk to the Provost Marshall. We had a Ferry at this point and another at a small place named Caroctin, five miles near Harpers Ferry. Our Ferry boat ran regular all day but the one at Caroctin made but two trips per day

Fig. 19. Jones' Landing, Virginia (vicinity). Pontoon bridge (open for steamers) across the James River, ca. 1861–1869. Library of Congress.

Fig. 20. Harper's Ferry, West Virginia. View of Maryland Heights, published 1865. James Gardner, 1832–?, photographer. Library of Congress.

with orders to permit no one to come or go but citizens who wanted to do trading. [See fig. 20.]

Our Regiment was encamped on a knoll about a quarter mile off from the station and the rows of tents presented a beautiful sight. Our orders were to permit certain persons to cross the river, those coming over to trade at the sutlers and those whom we thought had urgent calls to go south on business not connected with the Confederacy.

My business was to search suspected persons either coming or going, to see that they had no contraband goods and were not blockade runners. The first person desiring to cross and go south was a little Jew who dropped into the office one morning off the train.[5] "I have a werry seek prother in der sout" he said. We noticed that although he was a small man having thin arms and legs, his body was extra-large. My brother said, "Well if you have a sick brother south I guess you can go." The Jew smiled. "But George you had better take him upstairs and search him." He made all kinds of excuses to keep from going and after he was upstairs they were doubled "Mein Government" if

I removes mine cloding I will die wit cold on der spot." "Lettle boy you shust let it go und hers is a $5.00 bill. You say I was all right und you keep it for your own selluf." It was no good. I was too young to be bribed with five or ten or twenty five dollars. Well I found just sixty four pound of needles around Mr. Jew's body, done up in buckskins as neat as a pin. He and his needles were sent under guard to Baltimore which was the last we heard of him.[6]

A big lot of troops were in camp on Bolivar Heights at Harpers Ferry and they had caused the officers much trouble by getting drunk and fighting, etc. It was found that the whiskey was sent them in boxes by express by friends and dealers. The government ordered the Express Co. to leave all boxes etc., consigned to soldiers at Harpers Ferry at our station. We received orders to overhaul each and every box or package and confiscate what liquor it contained. It was quite a job but we managed it between other work. Nearly every box had more or less whiskey in it, and the devices resorted to, to keep it from being discovered were in many cases worthy of a better cause. Flasks of whiskey, as many as four in one loaf—were baked into bread. Cans were made to fit inside of other cans and the outside can filled with molasses. Bottles were buried in jars of butter, preserves etc. In fact every conceivable trick was tried but all failed except when there was a small bottle (half pint) which we would pass for medical use. All this liquor was kept in my room for weeks until we found that our own men were stealing it when we carried it all out and destroyed it. How those old bummers did hate to see such hilarity producing truck destroyed, and how they would like to have saved a few bottles. "What a shame," they cried, 'too bad.' It was no use. My brother was a strong temperance man, and so every last drop had to go.

Another Jew put in an appearance one day, when my brother was away and I was left to sign passes and attend to things for a few days. He was liberal with meerschaum pipes, presenting several officers who were loafing in the office, but I was of no account and I got no pipes nor was even was noticed by him. After awhile he wanted a pass across the river and the Jew was more than surprised to find out the he couldn't cross unless he had a pass from "that boy." He got none of course.[7]

Another chap we caught on horseback trying to bribe our guards and ferrymen to take him over. He was taken in charge. We allowed him his freedom thinking that his pony and bag of truck on each side would hold him, but he skipped in the night. One of his bags was full of meerschaum pipes and other full of fine cutlery. It began to look as though there was a demand for meerschaum pipes in the south.

The Cumberland Canal[8] ran through our town and along up the river past Harpers Ferry, although Harpers Ferry was on the opposite side of the river. The canal was used primarily for hauling coal from the mines at Cumberland. I am mentioning the canal only to tell how near I came to being drowned in it. It was only about twenty feet wide. Although I was only a lad, I was a good swimmer and had an idea—like other boys—that I could do anything. Some of our men liked whiskey pretty well and one day after they had been paid off, several of them got into a boat and were rowing up and down the canal. I was on my way over to the Ferry and in passing over the canal bridge I noticed a fellow fishing some distance up the bank. I walked up toward him to see what luck he was having. On my way, three parties whom I knew passed me in a boat; they were rowing as fast as possible, and were very reckless in their movements. I told them to be careful and one answered, "Oh we can't get drowned in this place." I saw they were full of liquor. They kept on and when about fifty yards away and while I was just about to stop and speak to the fisherman I heard a cry for help and looking up the canal I saw they were all in the water and floundering about. We both ran up to them. One man went down, another man struck bottom on the other side. I expected the man with me would jump in at once and try to save his friends but instead he was overcome with terror, and stood still ringing his hands and crying, "Oh! My God! Oh! My good Lord," whilst I had stripped and plunged into the water.[9] I caught the fellow by the arm trying to keep him from getting hold of me. As soon as he saw me he made desperate effort to get to me, but I went under the water and took him by the leg and tried to get him over to where his feet would touch the bottom which was only a couple of yards. I had no idea that he would sink again but he did and before I could get out of his way he had grasped me tight and I knew I was in the clutches of a man trying to save himself and without sense or mercy. I fought hard but to no purpose, death would not loosen his grip. I tried to get to the top of the water to breath. He was trying too, gulping down lots of water, but holding fast to me. I kept my presence of mind and kept my mouth closed until I thought my head was as big as a hogshead and then I thought I could breathe water. I guess as I opened my mouth but instead of air water ran into it and that's all I knew until I awoke in my room and heard a wild cheer from the outside. Two doctors had been doing their best and had succeeded. The soldiers thought I had been very brave and it was their cheer I had heard when they knew I had come back to earth. The other fellow was brought around quicker, not being as far gone as I was, having held himself up by pushing me under. It appears that the fellow who would not enter the water and try and rescue his comrades, had done the next best thing, he had aroused the camp by running back and shouting. My brother Joe, who was always first to any rescue, went running to know what the trouble was. As he came up, the fellow could only say, "Your brother George in there." It was enough. Joe had us out in a jiffy and the doctor was there in short order. The water was worked out of me and then I was rushed to my room and after more work I opened my eyes. I was much praised for my foolhardy attempt although this man a Frenchman (Pruno De Nice) would no doubt have been drowned had it not been for me. One poor fellow was drowned as it was. He was a German and use to bake our bread when we could procure flour instead of hard tack. I was soon well and out and around.

As I have before mentioned, there was a little place about three miles above on the railroad where a ferry was permitted to run only twice each day. Residents across the Potomac could come over and trade, but not strangers. If any came to this ferry the order was to tell them they could cross at Point of Rocks. A company from our regiment was stationed there under a Lieut. Benjamin. One evening a lady arrived at the other side who seemed to be well-supplied with money as she offered a big sum to the ferrymen to bring her over. They would not. But they told Lieut. Benjamin, who must have been awful hard up, and he sent them back for her. It afterwards came out that he got eighty dollars in gold from her. Twenty dollars for allowing her to cross. Twenty dollars for several other things, in all that amount eighty dollars. Well, in a few days we got word from Washington of what had occurred at Catoctin and Lieutenant Benjamin was ordered sent to Washington under arrest.[10] He was put into the old Capitol Prison but before his case came to trial, he took the small pox and died. The lady whom he had swindled so badly was the sister of the wife of one of our Cabinet Officers. We knew nothing of it until the arrest. My brother-in-law having been called to Washington on business, I was left to do much more than I ought. Hardly an officer could be trusted where a bribe was in sight, no matter how small and if only a meerschaum pipe.

One evening the last trip had been made by the ferryman to the other side taking back those who lived over there, and they remained longer than usual. Returning, they stated that they had been detained by a lady who had been left there by a teamster. She was all alone, no place to stay overnight and had nothing to eat. She implored them to bring her and her two big trunks over, offering any price. I could not permit a lady to remain on that barren shore over night so I sent them back for her. She soon arrived and was profuse in her thanks. I told her that she might have to go back south in the morning but I would see in the meantime. She was handsome, elegantly dressed and talked well. I had her trunks taken to the hotel and after supper I went over to examine them and her to see that she was or was not a blockade runner.

I went through her trunks. She had them full of fine clothing and among the rest was two stockings full to the top with jewelry of every kind. Diamond rings, watches, chains, etc. She had been one of the "Bourgeois" of the south and she stated that knowing Confederate money was of no value in the north, all of it she had and could get hold of she invested in jewelry and that is how she came by so much of it. I could find no good reason for putting this woman back across the river, so just before I retired I sent word to her that she would be permitted to take the train for the north whenever she felt disposed.

I was generally at the train when it arrived, in fact the train passed at our station. I was busy watching express boxes put off when someone touched my arm and turning about there was my lady. She handed me a small package wrapped in a piece of paper, saying "a small memento for your kindness." I said thank you and good bye, and as there was a crowd around I thrust the little package into my vest pocket. I thought to myself, here is a dollar or two that she had better keep herself, I had more money than I knew where to spend it, and would sooner not have had money that I thought someone needed worse than myself. I was busy that day and forgot my package until after supper when I pulled it out and opening it was surprised to find I had a most beautiful diamond ring with thirteen beautiful stones. A Captain McComas was standing by me when I opened it. "I will give you two hundred dollars for it," said he, but I would not sell. It was large for me so I had cord wrapped about it to make it fit me. I know that many parties envied me this ring and wanted it badly and some of them would have waylaid me for it if they had been sure of getting it. Instead of sending it home I wore it continually like a young "gump" that I was. I slept under blankets, and the setting of the ring would get caught in them when I wore it at night, so I use to remove it on retiring and place it on my washstand which stood at the head of my bed. I was very particular about placing it on my finger the first thing after arising in the morning. But one morning, just as I reached the place where I boarded-which was about two blocks from my sleeping room, I found that I had overlooked my ring. I hurried back, running part of the way, but I was too late, the ring was gone. I felt awfully bad about it and cried. It was no use, it was gone and I never saw nor heard of it again.

About three years after I did expect I would hear from it. The man who I almost knew for a certainty had stolen it, died, and thought he would say something about it. I believe he would had it still been in his possession, but he was a "fast" chap and I think has either given it to some woman, or had sold it in order to make expenses.

It took me a long time to recover from the loss of this ring. It certainly was a thing of beauty and being young and giddy I thought I was "some pumpkin" when I had that flashing, sparkling, gandy bauble on my hand.

I had another diamond since then. A nice stone valued at two hundred dollars or more. I carried it in my big wallet wrapped in a wad of cotton. I lost that I know not how. I went to show it one day, but it was gone, gone, gone,! I have never seen it and never expect to.

The Baltimore and Ohio Canal follows the Baltimore and Ohio Railroad along its way up to the Cumberland coal region. Most all the hauling is coal. From Point of Rocks to Harpers Ferry the canal and railroad run close together following the Potomac River around the base of the mountains. At one time the mountains came down to the water's edge as below: [see fig. 21]. Then the railroad and canal cut their way through like this: [see fig. 22]. Just above Point of Rocks and where the railroad had begun to cut its way around the mountain, an immense rock had been left above on the mountain side. At the time the rebels were destroying as much of this railroad as they could conveniently get at, after very much labor they moved this immense stone to the edge of the bluff and sent it crashing down onto the track.

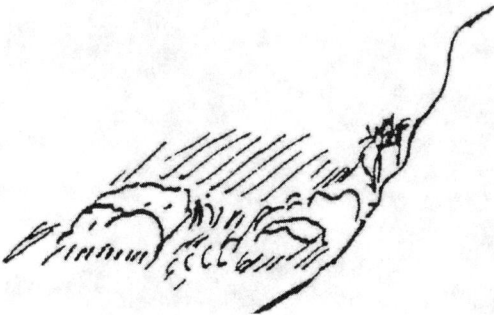

Fig. 21. Mountains to water sketch by George Maguire.

Fig. 22. Rail canal sketch by George Maguire.

It certainly destroyed the tracks, as the twisted rails that stuck up out of the canal attested. But that was all the harm it done and it done a very good turn for the railroad company. The big stone was so heavy that it went down into the earth far enough to allow the top to come even with the road bed, and all the company had to do was to lay their new track over this solid foundation and go ahead. The rails which could not be pulled out from beneath with a locomotive were bent back close to the rock and made an excellent place to tie boats. [See fig. 23.]

From Point of Rocks to Harpers Ferry is about twelve miles or so.

Fig. 23. Harper's Ferry, West Virginia. View of the town and railroad bridge. From the main eastern theater of the war, Battle of Antietam, September–October 1862. Library of Congress.

We had some captured horses which we wanted to turn into the department quartermaster at Harpers Ferry. So I and our colored man and another chap rode them up there one afternoon. After transacting the business, I sent the Negro back on the train and in time to getting his mess supper. A lieutenant was the "other chap" and we loitered until too late for the 4 p.m. train and just then a canal boat came along. "Let's take passage," said I and we got aboard. It was then about 5:00 p.m. We arrived at Point of Rocks the next morning. After running until dark the boat was hauled up close to the bank and tied. We had supper and the mules had theirs and after a short talk we all turned in. My friend and I slept undercover and on a lot of hay. I slept soundly and sweetly. In the morning we had breakfast and then got underway and by eight or nine o'clock were home. It was slow moving but being a change I enjoyed it, but when one is in a hurry they want to go by another route. We had no charges to pay. All free.

Time came when the Regiment was ordered to more active duties and I was again in Baltimore.

My brother-in-law went back to Harpers Ferry and then to Winchester[11] where he was taken a prisoner and taken to Richmond and put into Libby Prison.[12] He was there for almost a year and was exchanged finally and came home.[13] [See fig. 24.]

Fig. 24. Harper's Ferry, photographed immediately after its evacuation by the Rebels, 1861. C. O. Bostwick, photographer. Library of Congress.

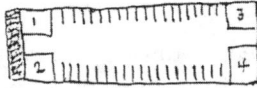

CHAPTER 5

RETURN TO BALTIMORE: HICKS UNITED STATES GENERAL HOSPITAL

After returning to Baltimore I spent time between that city Annapolis and my sisters' farm in Anne Arundel County Maryland. There was some excitement at all times in Baltimore. One time it was reported that a noted guerilla was on his way to capture the city.[1] Excitement ran high. From one end of the city to the other the cross streets were blockaded.[2] Hogsheads filled with dirt were stood on end close up to each other, then big scanting were run over the top and pieces laid on top. It made a very good breastwork, but all the good it did was to cause sale for all the old empty hogshead in Baltimore.

When the President would call for more soldiers, a certain number would be called from each state as to its population. The state officers would then divide up the number between the counties in the state, also according to population and then the officers of the different counties or cities would put the names of all able-bodied men between twenty one and forty five years of age into a big box. A blind person or someone blindfolded would then draw out as many men names as required. Men who were thus "drafted" would have to go into the army or furnish a "substitute." The daily papers were also full of advertisements for "substitutes," as high as $1500 being offered. One party offered in case his substitute was wounded and permanently disabled, to provide for him during life, or in case of being killed to give him decent burial, poor consolation. Many or I might say, all the states offered "bounties" of from $300 to $1000 to men in order to make up their quota without drafting. A class of men-hard cases were formed called "Bounty jumpers." Men who would enlist and get the bounty and at the first opportunity would escape or desert

and then enlist for another bounty. There was a great many men who
got good big pay for enlisting that went to the front. Old soldiers did
not take kindly to these men who enlisted for money and many of
them had a hard time of it on that account. Any number of foreigners
went into the army for the money in it and served through the war.[3]

After I had been in Baltimore for five or six months I got very tired
of doing little or nothing, so one day, in company with a young fellow
that I use to run with we went down to an office where there was a
sign out "Highest prices paid for Substitutes," and offered ourselves.
The fellow in charge took us around to a recruiting office to have us
examined. We were ushered into a big room, where there was a dozen
or so of naked men being examined. The Doctor looked at me and said
"Have you your mother's consent?" "No sir," I said. "Go home and get
it and then I'll examine you." My friend was old enough but he would
never go unless I would, so the substitute broker said after we got outside, "Come let us go up on Holiday Street there is another officer there
and maybe they will accept you." Away we went and were shown into
a room where there were two Doctors. One took me in charge and
the other took my friend. My doctor looked into my eyes and said to
the other "Cornea badly affected and cannot be accepted." Then said
the other, "They are very particular now." Turning to me he said, "Not
accepted," and I marched out. In a minute out came my friend. "Why
didn't you go in?" I asked. "Oh! I wasn't going without you," so we
turned our steps towards home. I to find that the whole of my family
were out on the warpath after me, someone having told them I had
gone off to enlist. This was the closest I ever came to going as a soldier
and it wasn't my fault that I didn't go.[4]

One day as I was walking about I met a young fellow named Howard
whom I went to school with. I found that he was employed as a nurse
in one of the numerous hospitals in Baltimore. He said, "There is a
new hospital being erected in the western part of the city. I and my
brother have both got promises of a position there and we are to go
there next week. Come with us. Make application and I am almost sure
you can get a place. Wages $40 and board." Well, I made application as
an "experienced nurse" and got a place very soon. The Hospital was
planned by a Surgeon named "Hicks" and was named after him "Hicks
U.S. Hospital."

I took up my quarters with the two Howard boys. We camped in
tents on the grounds as the hospital was not finished, and for two or
three months we had nothing to do but eat and sleep. The Howard
boys were selfish and treated me uncommonly mean, because they

knew how things should be done and I did not, and as I had to know I was compelled to take any meanness until I learned that I could get along without them.

The Hospital was finally finished and I think it was the most complete of any Hospital built during the war.[5] The plan was like this: [see fig. 25].[6]

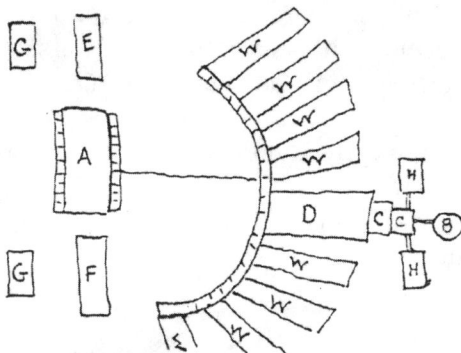

Fig. 25. Hicks hospital layout sketch
by George Maguire.

A. was the Administration building where all the clerical work was done, supplies kept. Surgeons Apartments, Apothecary, Printing office, Rooms for wounded officers etc. 2 stories[7]

W. Were Wards arranged in half circle. There was 20 of them. 10 on each side of the dining hall. They all fronted on a wide covered walk which extended to all without a break. There was 60 beds in each ward. The Wards were arranged like this: [see fig. 26].

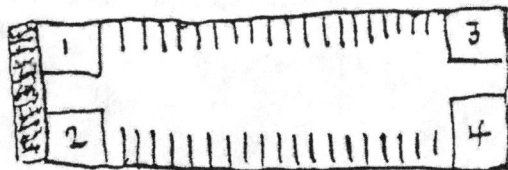

Fig. 26. Hospital ward layout sketch
by George Maguire.

1. Baggage Room
2. Ward master's Room
3. Water Closet and washroom; having soap stone and marble fixings.
4. Was a furnace room. A big furnace in here was supposed to heat

each ward by steam heat. The wards were but one story, well lighted and ventilated. Cots were arranged on each side. 30 on a side.[8]

D. Dining hall 2 stories. A very large building having room for six tables across it and running the full length. When the bell rang, all parties able to walk would fall into line on the veranda in front of their respective Wards, with the Ward master in front, and at the next ring of the bell would march to the hall. If a Ward was not ready, they had to wait until all the others had filed past and fall in behind. The food was good and plentiful. Patients who could not get up had their food brought to them and many had extra diet prescribed. A bill of fare was printed every day, and the diet suitable for each patient was picked out for them.[9]

B.C. and H.H. were Cook house, Bakery, Laundry, Engine and Boiler rooms, etc.[10]

E. was a drug store room[11]

F. The operating room[12]

G. G. Were quarters for Clerks and Hospital Stewards[13]

I was awfully timid about the dead when I went to the hospital. I was looking around one day, after I had been there a few days and coming to the building marked E I looked in. It was quite a long room. The windows were all closed with shutters and the only light it got was from the door at which I was standing. I entered and walked down nearly to the other end. A cart was standing to one side or as we called it a "stretcher." It was covered with a sheet. I went over and raised the sheet to see what was there and to say that I was scared merely would be putting it light. A dead man was lying there. Had been left until a grave could be dug. So as soon as I saw that it was a dead man I made a break for the door. It was a mad rush with the thought that someone was behind me and about to catch hold of me. I bounced through that open door like a cannon ball shot out of a gun. I think had someone closed that door whilst I was on the run I would have crashed through it.

I got over that before I left the hospital and was no more timid about the dead than if they were so much clay, as they really were. I remember going down to the "Dead House" at two o'clock at night to get the stretcher to remove a dead man. It was a dark night; the place was a quarter mile from the hospital in a piece of timber. I was alone and had to go in where there was two or three dead and more or less dissected, without any light, and feel and shuffle around to find the stretcher. I was not in the least afraid. This shows that a person can be habituated to almost anything.

The hospital was finally completed and the patients from all the other hospitals were brought to it. The Howard boys were astonished and showed much chagrin when an order was handed me to take charge of Ward Ten as Ward Master with ten dollars more salary per month beside the honor. They both went to the chief surgeon and told them that I was inexperienced as a nurse whilst they knew it all. I was summoned to appear before the surgeon and I went, expecting to at least lose the position of Ward Master. There were three surgeons in the room when I entered. They asked me a number of questions and the Chief asked me a question about a little fuzz that was beginning to sprout on my upper lip. I do not remember my answer but I know they all roared with laughter. "You'll do," said the Chief and that was all the good it done them. Beside I got acquainted with these doctors and was quite intimate with all of them afterwards, being invited to several entertainments gotten up for them.

The Howard boys were very angry but I went along my own way. One of the Doctors wanted to put one of them in my Ward under me, but I knew he wouldn't like it, so I objected. They were made more envious when they heard I had been appointed a "Medical Cadet" with more salary. I was the youngest Ward Master in the hospital and that was what hurt the others. I had a superior education, made up my reports in good shape, was polite and gentlemanly-never envious-and attended strictly to duty. [See fig. 27.]

Fig. 27. Hicks U.S. General Hospital, Baltimore, Maryland, 1861. Lithograph printed in colors by E. Sachse & Co., 1861. Hambleton Print Collection, Special Collections Department. Courtesy of the Maryland Historical Society, Item ID: H372.

I had six nurses under me and they understood their work and did it well without never a word for me. The patients were all wounded men whose wounds were bad ones. One man—a New York gambler before entering the army—had a bad wound in the leg below the knee. The Surgeon wanted to amputate his leg, but no, he would die but his leg must not be taken off. He was a small man, weighing when in health about 120lbs., but now he was less than 100lbs. His leg from the knee down to his foot was as large as four legs. It was kept in a box and had great deep holes which were green and would fill up with puss twice each day. It was a nasty job to dress it, but I had a nurse who was equal to it. His leg in the box was like this: [see fig. 28]. The indentations were from an inch to two inches deep. The leg was always covered except when being dressed. It was erysipelas.[14] Time and time again he was advised to have it off, but he wouldn't hear to it. Finally the disease began getting above the knee. We sent to New York for his wife. She came and advised him to let his leg go. One afternoon he sent for me and said "I have made up my mind to let that old leg go. I have held onto it for a long while but it's no use, I find I cannot get well with it, so if you will make arrangements I will have it off tomorrow morning." So I started to make the arrangements. In about an hour his wife came into my room and said she thought her husband was getting worse. I went out to see him and at once summoned the doctor. He stated that my man was in a precarious condition, that the erysipelas had gone too far. He ordered the upper part above the knee bandaged tightly and as he was going he whispered to me "Your man

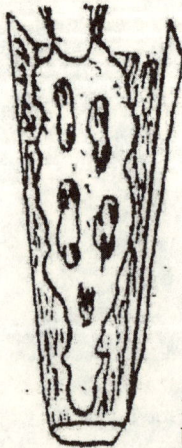

Fig. 28. Diseased leg sketch by George Maguire.

will not live to see the next sunrise." And sure enough at about 11:00 p.m. he died. We wanted that leg for a specimen but his wife objected. We got it anyway. We had the carpenter fashion a wood one and we took the leg and substituted the wood. He died to keep his leg and lost it after giving his life for it.

I was the only ward master that was capable of prescribing diet, so the Doctor said, and that was how I got to be "Medical Cadet." I couldn't prescribe diet without a title and so I got it.[15] I had many bad cases in my ward, in fact all the worst cases. I had a man from Maine named Leonard. He had been shot through the foot, the ball going into his heel and coming out just at the base of his toes. He too dreaded to lose his foot and for months he had lain there hoping against the impossible, as the bones in his foot had all been splintered.

One morning he called me as I was passing and said "I had a dream last night and I am going to test it. I dreamed that I had had my foot taken off and that it was only a week until I was on my way home. If you will attend to it, I am ready anytime to be taken to the operating room." Before noon his foot was off and he was back on his cot. The Doctor had told me time and again that this man would never have his foot well and it was folly for him to expect it and so I had persuaded to have it done, but he waited for his dream. The queerest thing was that on the very day one week from the day his foot was amputated he was on his way home. A happy man seemingly.

I got very tired of being around where so many nasty wounds and sores were continually in the light, where so much sickness and suffering were always present, and I felt as if prescribing diet to sick was not just my forte, yet I had no just cause for complaint. I had been treated so well by everyone that I could but do what everyone asked to have done. I had in my ward a tall fine-looking man by the name of Murphy. He was undoubtedly a handsome Irish man. He talked very little, wanted very little and was so quiet and reserved that I hardly knew he was in the ward. I was in the wash room one afternoon when he came in coughing and in a moment began gulping up great mouthfuls of blood. He kept it up until a bucket was over half full of great pieces of blood in the form of jelly, quivering as jelly does. I was almost horror-struck at the sight, but managed to get some salt and get him to swallow a little which he did not want to do. When through he washed his mouth, went back to his cot without a word and never arose from it again. A few days after he was taken with another hemorrhage but was too weak to throw off the blow and so died. As he lay on his cot, white as a piece of marble, I thought he was as handsome a six foot specimen of humanity as I ever saw, and I wondered if there was not some friend who would have given much to have been near him and soothed his last moments.

Next to my ward was the "Private Disease" Hospital in which were some of the most loathsome affected men of the army.[16] Next to Leprosy I think their diseases the worst. On the other side was the "Colored" ward. One poor fellow in that ward was peculiarly affected. T'was said that he had been bitten by a rabid dog. Anyhow every other day he would have a spell and get down on his hands and knees and bark and go on precisely like a dog in distress. The Ward Master would tie him whenever a fit was coming on. He would come and let it be known and asked to be tied. Although so unfortunate, the convalescents would have lots of amusement with him. He would snap at anything held near him like a dog and would froth at the mouth and roll his eyes most frightfully. I wondered that he would come out of such "spells," which he did in an hour or so, utterly exhausted, so that he would have to go at once to bed, being too weak to sit or stand. I have often thought of what disposition was made of him after the hospital closed. Buried in the government insane asylum perhaps.

We had another poor fellow there called "Jack." Whether that was his name or he or anyone knew his right name I could never discover. He was a very large man. A two hundred pounder about. A red-headed, red-bearded Irishman, I think. He was nearly always skipping like a school boy-sidewise-from one end of the grounds to the other, nearly always on the go. Every grind of tobacco he would find he would push into a mouth already as full as it could hold and should one stop and ask him a question, ten chances to one he would let the whole mouthful fly over you in his effort to laugh. He would laugh and then discovering he had lost his mouthful of old grinds he would gaze at them sorrowfully and unless prevented would pick them up again. When prevented he would turn and skip away, stopping whenever a grind met his sight. He was as harmless as a kitten, poor fellow, although as big and having the strength of a giant almost. Many months after the hospital closed I was at the Baltimore Alms house[17] and whilst out in the yard I saw a big man, red headed and red bearded, dressed in garment resembling a long night shirt-go skipping down by the side of a high wall. I overtook him and as I thought, it was "Jack" same as ever, with his mouth full of old grinds I did not get him to laugh. I was standing talking to a young fellow sometime after and as we talked Jack went skipping down by the side of a high board fence. Without thinking to hit him, the young fellow picked up a stone and threw it and I saw it hit poor Jack in the forehead. It did not hit him square, but glanced. I saw Jack stop suddenly like he was astonished. Then as the blood ran down into his eyes, he shook his head like an animal and went on skipping. This man had been a soldier. Whether he was enlisted as an imbecile or became after enlistment through sickness I could not learn.[18] I know that he was entitled to a pile of money, and why he was in an alms house was hard to understand. He may be there yet. In any event it makes little difference to him I suppose.

Just about the time I was getting heartily tired of the monotony of being a Ward Master as I would have been tired of any other position, I was detailed as "Property Clerk" and that changed my quarters to the big building. It took me out from among the sick and wounded and thereafter I had little or nothing to do with that department. I also changed my eating and sleeping quarters. The hospital stewards and clerks had an extra "Mess" and a building to themselves for sleeping. I liked the change. I was property clerk for a while and then went to the "Living room," having charge of all linen and the Laundry Department. Besides the Laundry (a big affair) and the linen room (another big affair) I had all the Sanitary Commission goods to look after, that was all stuff sent for the sick and wounded. Preserves, jellies, canned goods, pickles etc. and extra clothing, bandages etc. I had become an important person, but did not get the "big head" a bit. I was too young in the first place and I saw so much of "big-headed" people that I had no desire to be classed among them or called one.

There was quite a number of ladies employed and most of them were in my department. One in charge of the laundry girls, one in the "Commission" room and two in the Living Room. I was on good terms with all of them and had a nice time. I lost sight of the Howard's after going out of my ward, and do not remember much of them after that time, only that they had said to some of my young friends that I had become so "high toned that I would not look at a common person." That was not so, unless the person had shown themselves to be so very common (as they did).[19]

I finally got to doing almost as it pleased me. An inventory of drugs on hand was called for and I took the job of doing it. Having a faculty for spelling correctly I consequently made a good report of what would have been impossible to most of our clerks, who were an inferior lot at the best. This work gave me a "reputation" and thereafter I was asked to do only nice work and very little. I had a fine time, being at liberty to go out whenever disposed. But all things have an ending and so did our Hospital. I was very sorry to lose my good occupation and part with my salary etc. The order was out, all those finely-built and splendidly-arranged buildings must be vacated, torn down, everything sold at auction and swept as it were, off the face of the earth.

Things were sold awfully cheap, almost given away, but that made little difference to Uncle Sam. We got our last pay check and the good days spent at "Hicks U.S. General Hospital" were a thing of the past.[20]

A visit to where this Hospital was located a year later showed only a barren field. Not a vestige of anything approaching a house was visible. A pile of dirt here and there, with a few broken brick was all that remained. After leaving the hospital I returned to my home. The war was over and the review of the returned soldiers was to be held in Washington D.C. Why I did not go down there I do not know, but I missed a sight I would like very much to have in memory.

CONCLUSION

In addition to adding to the growing body of primary sources chronicling the experience of children and youth's in the American Civil War, Maguire's narrative also provides the opportunity to consider memory, and how Americans remembered the American Civil War. Historian David Thelan argues that "memory, private and individual as much as collective and cultural, is constructed and not reproduced. This construction is not made in isolation but in conversations with others that occur in the contexts of community, broader politics, and social dynamics. In the study of memory the important question is not how accurately a recollection fitted some piece of a past reality, but why historical actors constructed their memories in a particular way at a particular time."[1] Maguire wrote his memoir twenty eight years after the war ended. With this in mind, it is difficult to know why it took him so long, but less difficult to understand why he finally wrote it in the first place.

Literature on the Civil War began to circulate in 1861 shortly after the first shots were fired on Fort Sumter. Collectively the literature embodied many different topics and ideals as the war played out across the nation. Union and Confederate participants, the initial chroniclers, had a common purpose. They generally strove to justify their cause, while they celebrated the bravery and courage of their comrades. After 1865, the primary motive was celebration. At the end of the nineteenth century, the dwindling battalion of survivors found a shared identity as "band of brothers" and the theme of most common war literature reflected the political desire of reconciliation and the efforts of the reconstruction era.[2] The 1880s proved a time period during which massive amounts of literature was being published about the war. "Books, newspapers, magazines serials, and the conflicts official documents. Much of the material was military in nature —descriptive accounts of battles, fictional portraits of soldiers coming to grips with the war, biographies and memoirs of soldiers, unit histories – and it fed the public's insatiable appetite."[3]

We don't have any evidence of what Maguire might have read. We do not know if he read literature relating to the war. We do not know if he read the memoir of Ulysses S. Grant, or the works on Robert E. Lee by Jubal A. Early. We don't know if he was aware of the southern textbook crusade throughout the south that sought to redefine the meaning of the war along the lines of the "Lost Cause" ideology. We do not know if he was he influenced by the popular fiction authors of his age who emphasized the ethos of white reconciliation and white unity that emerged after the war. These questions and more can never be definitively answered, but his effort does suggest that in writing this memoir, Maguire knew he was making history and contributing to the growing body of knowledge related to the American Civil War.

Following the battle of Antietam, the Maryland 5th Infantry Regiment was assigned to General Milroy's Division and besieged at Winchester. The regiment then rejoined the army of the Potomac in 1864 and participated in the siege of Petersburg June to September 1864 and was with that part of the Army of the Potomac known as 3d Brigade, 2d Division, 18th Army Corps, and the 2nd Brigade, 3rd Division, 24th Army Corps that occupied Richmond, Va. on April 3, 1865. On May 23–24, 1865 both the Union Army, led by Ulysses S. Grant, and the Army of the Potomac, led by George Gordon Meade participated in the Grand Review of the Armies that celebrated the close of the Civil War.[4] There is no doubt that members of the Maryland 5th were in attendance and marched in the parade. Many of their members can also be found on Grand Army of the Republic (GAR) registries in states all over the country.[5] The regiment was mustered out of the military service of the United States at Fredericksburg, Va., September 1, 1865, and transported thence to Baltimore, Md., where the regiment disbanded.[6]

Beyond the *History and Roster of the Maryland Volunteers, 1861–1865,* found in the *Official Records of the War,* no expanded history on the Volunteer Maryland Fifth Infantry Regiment exists. Hopefully this memoir will contribute to a future endeavor on that front.

As for the life of George C. Maguire following the war, there is record to suggest he stayed in Maryland through 1870. The 1870 United States Federal census shows a George C. McGuire, age 23, living in the household of Salome Marsh in Baltimore City, Ward 7.[7] There are additional census and marriage records that suggest he went west sometime after 1870, married in Missouri, and then went on to live in Sabetha, Kansas where he worked and raised two children. There is also a George Campbell Maguire buried in the Forest Lawn Memorial

Park in Omaha, Nebraska with a birth date of January 26, 1847, and a death date of January 15, 1908. A look through census and marriage records strongly suggests it is the same man who wrote this memoir, but the work of a genealogists is needed to undertake a search process linked to the Maguire social and familial networks to construct meaning from, frame and confirm the data.[8] His personal history will flesh out from within the Maguire family "'Community of Record,' with a genealogical search for records and the construction of meaning by a genealogist through their interactions with the records, their families, family archives and other genealogists."[9]

The original memoir remains in the care of Maguire's great grandson in Homestead, Florida. A copy of the original can also be found in the archives at the Antietam National Battle Field in Sharpsburg, Maryland.

NOTES

Introduction

1. 1850, 1860, United States Federal Census.
2. Frederick Henry Dyer, *A Compendium of the War of the Rebellion* (New York: T. Yoseloff, 1959), 1235; L. Allison Wilmer, J. H. Jarrett and Geo. W. F. Vernon, *History and Roster of Maryland Volunteers, War of 1861–6 Volume 1*, Vol 367 (Baltimore, MD: Guggenheimer, Well, & Co., 1899), 187–89.
3. Scott Sheads and Daniel Carroll Toomey, *Baltimore during the Civil War* (Linthicum, MD: Toomey Press, 1997), 12–13.
4. Ibid., 30–31.
5. For work on how the Civil War was remembered and memory in general, see David Thelan, *Memory and American History* (Bloomington and Bloomington: Indiana University Press, 1990); Joan Waugh and Alice Fahs, eds., *The Memory of the Civil War in American Culture* (Chapel Hill: University of North Carolina Press, 2004); David W. Blight, *Race and Reunion: the Civil War in American Memory* (Cambridge, MA: Belknap Press of Harvard University Press, 2001); Caroline E. Janney, *Remembering the Civil War: Reunion and the Limits of Reconciliation* (Chapel Hill: University of North Carolina Press, 2013); Brian Craig Miller, *John Bell Hood and the Fight for Civil War Memory* (Knoxville: University of Tennessee Press, 2010); Anne Sarah Rubin, *Through the Heart of Dixie: Sherman's March and American Memory* (Chapel Hill: University of North Carolina Press, 2014); Benjamin Cloyd, *Haunted by Atrocity: Civil War Prisons in American Memory* (Baton Rouge: Louisiana State University Press, 2010).
6. Charles Pierce Roland, *An American Iliad: The Story of the Civil War* (Lexington: University Press of Kentucky, 1991). 54.
7. Dyer, *A Compendium of the War of Rebellion*, 1235.
8. Ibid., 1235.
9. Sheads and Toomey, *Baltimore during the Civil War*, 52.
10. Ibid., 148.
11. Required reading for studies on the topic of children and youth during the Civil War–era include James A. Marten, *Lessons of War: The Civil War in Children's Magazines* (Wilmington, DE: SR Books, 1999); James A. Marten, *Children for the Union: The War Spirit on the Northern Home Front* (Chicago: Ivan R. Dee, 2004); James A. Marten, *Children and Youth During the Civil War Era* (New York: New York University Press, 2012); James A. Marten, "For the

Good, the True, and the Beautiful: Northern Children's Magazines and the Civil War," *Civil War History* 41 (Mar. 1995): 57–75; James A. Marten, "Stern Realities: Children of Chancellorsville and Beyond," in *Chancellorsville: The Battle and Its Aftermath*, ed. Gary W. Gallagher (Chapel Hill and London: University of North Carolina Press, 1996), 219–43; James A. Marten, "Fatherhood in the Confederacy: Southern Soldiers and Their Children," *Journal of Southern History* 63 (May 1997): 269–92. Additional work on the topic include Peter W. Bardaglio, "The Children of Jubilee: African-American Childhood in Wartime," in *Divided Houses: Gender and the Civil War*, ed. Catherine Clinton and Nina Silber (New York and Oxford: Oxford University Press, 1992), 213–29; Ronald E. Butchart, *Schooling the Freed People: Teaching, Learning, and the Struggle for Black Freedom, 1861–1876* (Chapel Hill: University of North Carolina Press, 2010); Catherine Clinton, "Orphans of the Storm," in her *Civil War Stories* (Athens and London: University of Georgia Press, 1998), 42–80; Elizabeth Daniels, "The Children of Gettysburg," in *American Heritage* 40 (May–June 1989): 97–107; Edmund L. Drago, *Confederate Phoenix: Rebel Children and their Families in South Carolina* (New York: Fordham University Press, 2008); Anya Jabour, *Topsy-Turvy: How the Civil War Turned the World Upside Down for Southern Children* (Chicago: Ivan R. Dee, 2010); Victoria E. Ott, *Confederate Daughters: Coming of Age during the Civil War* (Carbondale: Southern Illinois University Press, 2008); Rebecca J. Scott, "The Battle over the Child: Child Apprenticeship and the Freedmen's Bureau in North Carolina," in *Growing Up in America: Children in Historical Perspective*, ed. N. Ray Hiner and Joseph M. Hawes (Urbana: University of Illinois Press, 1985), 193–207; Emily E. Werner, *Reluctant Witnesses: Children's Voices from the Civil War* (New York: Westview Press, 1998). To follow existing and emerging scholarship on the history of childhood and youth, visit the Society for the History of Childhood and Youth website at www.shcy.org.

12. Steven Mintz, *Huck's Raft: A History of American Adolescenthood* (Cambridge, MA: Belknap Press of Harvard University Press, 2004), 118.

1. From Baltimore to the Peninsula Campaign with the Fifth Maryland Infantry Regiment

1. Maguire is speaking of the Constitutional Union Party, which was formed chiefly of the remnants of the Know-Nothings, the southern wing of the Whig Party, and other southern groups. At the founding convention held in Baltimore, Maryland in May 1860, the party nominated former U.S. Sen. John Bell of Tennessee for president and Edward Everett of Massachusetts for vice president. The formation of the party was prompted by the desire to muster popular sentiment in favor of the Union, and against southern secession. Doris Kearns Goodwin, *Team of Rivals: The Political Ge-*

nius of *Abraham Lincoln* (New York, NY: Simon and Schuster, 2005), 259. For more on politics, see Jean H. Baker, *The Politics of Continuity: Maryland Political Parties from 1858 to 1870* (Baltimore, MD: Johns Hopkins University Press, 1973).

2. The city possessed extensive shipping lines, railroads, and roads that connected it to the nation's capital, other major cities, and the oceans of the world. The shipping lines and railroads that brought goods in and out of the city brought politicians and delegates in and out as well. Travel between Baltimore and Washington was easy. There was also an ample supply of hotels, inns, and meeting places. As a result, the population of Baltimore was very politically active. Sheads and Toomey, *Baltimore during the Civil War*, 1–3.

3. A common misconception in 1861 and today is that Baltimoreans as a whole were opposed to Federal control and were of the same mind to attack any Federal opposition. An analysis of the Pratt Street riot and the early conflict on the streets of Baltimore at the beginning of the war reveal that many people, both black and white, sought to aid the Federal forces. Maguire's perspective and the descriptions of his brother-in-law's activities and political sentiment also reinforce this. Sheads and Toomey, *Baltimore during the Civil War*, 3. For more on Baltimore during the Civil War, see Harry A. Ezratty, *Baltimore in the Civil War: The Pratt Street Riot and a City Occupied* (Charleston, SC: History Press, 2010); Elizabeth Fee, Linda Shopes, and Linda Zeidman, *The Baltimore Book: New Views of Local History* (Philadelphia: Temple University Press, 1991).

4. Baltimore's exact position between North and South produced a combination of northern business affiliations with a distinct southern society to create a free fire zone of political debate that may not have been possible in either a northern or southern state. The steady diet of conventions kept Baltimoreans politically active on all levels. The high level of energy exhibited on Election Day in Baltimore City led to the city acquiring the nick name Mob Town. Sheads and Toomey, *Baltimore during the Civil War*, 4.

5. Baltimore spawned a chapter of the Republican Party known as the Wide Awakes. Active members of this chapter marched to rallies wearing green capes and slate-covered caps with red trim. During the Lincoln campaign the Wide Awakes staged a torchlight procession that wound up at the Holliday Street Theatre. Robert J. Brugger, *Maryland, A Middle Temperament, 1634–1980* (Baltimore, MD: Johns Hopkins University Press, in association with the Maryland Historical Society, 1988), 269.

6. The Bell-Air Market was situated in Old Town between Gay and Lord Streets in downtown Baltimore. It was built around 1835. Charles A. Varle, *A Complete View of Baltimore With a Statistical Sketch of all the Commercial, Mercantile, Manufacturing, Literary, Scientific, and Religious Institutions and Establishments, In the Same, and In Its Vicinity for Fifteen Miles Round, Derived from*

Personal Observation and Research into the Most Authentic Sources of Information
(Baltimore: S. Young, 1833), 39.

7. Maryland voted against Lincoln in the election of 1860. The number of
votes per candidate statewide was as follows: Breckinridge, 42,497, Bell,
41,177, Douglas, 5,873, and Lincoln, 2,300. Sheads and Toomey, *Baltimore
during the Civil War*, 6. See also Lawrence M. Denton, *A Southern Star for
Maryland: Maryland and the Secession Crisis, 1860–1861*, first edition (Baltimore, MD: Publishing Concepts, 1995).

8. The president elect's train was scheduled to arrive in Baltimore on February 22. Lincoln was re-routed after his head of security, Allan Pinkerton,
and Secretary of State William H. Seward advised against passage through
Baltimore. Rumors of a rebel assassination plot convinced the three that
avoiding Baltimore was the best course of action. Lincoln arrived safely
in Washington on February 23, while Mrs. Lincoln, their three sons, and
Lincoln's private secretary, John Hay, visited the city. Talk of the conspir-
acy created hostile feelings towards Baltimore from the rest of the country
and reinforced rebel sentiment within the city. The Midnight Ride, as this
passage came to be called, was later regretted by President Lincoln. For a
more explicit account of Lincoln's Midnight Ride through Baltimore, see
George William Brown, *Baltimore and the 19th of April 1861: A Study of the War*
(Baltimore, MD: Johns Hopkins University Press, 2001), 17–20.

9. As the war began events in Baltimore moved quickly. On April 12, Confederate batteries opened fire on Major Robert Anderson's command at Fort
Sumter. President Lincoln responded by calling for 75,000 volunteers to
put down the rebellion. Two days later Virginia passed an Ordinance of
Secession. All eyes were then on Maryland, which remained divided in
her loyalties. The city of Baltimore best exemplified the root of that division. On the north side of the city stood an industrial center, whose
predominantly western European labor force helped to abolish slavery
organically. On the south of the city farms and plantations operated with
slave labor that fed the demands of international markets. In 1860, Maryland as a whole contained 83,942 free people of color, 87,189 slaves, and a
white population of 515,918. This was a very different ratio of free to slave
and black to white compared to other southern states in the same year.
As a border state the divided loyalties were further complicated, and the
position of Maryland was critical: the nation's capital was surrounded on
three sides by Maryland, and all the roads from the North leading to it
passed through Maryland territory. Sheads and Toomey, *Baltimore during
the Civil War*, 13; Brown, *Baltimore and the 19th of April*, 30–37.

10. The Palmetto flag was the South Carolina state flag. It became the very
symbol of secession after South Carolina was the first state to secede from
the Union in December of 1860. The Rattle Snake flag traces its roots
to the Minute Men of the Revolutionary War and signified resistance to

Great Britain. The Rattle Snake flag was raised again when the Minute Men were activated as a unit in the Confederacy. Marc Leepson, *The Flag: An American Biography* (New York: Thomas Dunn Books/St. Martin's Press, 2005), 100–104. For more on Confederates in Maryland, see Daniel D. Hartzler, *Marylanders in the Confederacy* (Westminster, MD: Family Line Publications, 1986).

11. In July of 1861 Gen. John A. Dix took command of the area to encompass New Jersey, Pennsylvania, Virginia, and the Eastern Shore counties of Maryland. In securing Baltimore, he immediately forbade the display of the Confederate colors, and on September 4, 1861, he forbade the sale and display of secession badges along with any other emblem of the Confederacy. Sheads and Toomey, *Baltimore during the Civil War*, 46.

12. The night before the Pratt Street riot a State Rights Convention was held in Baltimore. The convention delegates condemned the actions of President Lincoln against the southern states and passed a round of resolutions to that effect, but they did not advocate secession. The resolutions also did not advocate attacks on troops but a careful reading of them may reveal the source of Maguire's memory of abolitionists ordered to leave the city. One resolution calls for "all good citizens to unite in a common effort to obliterate all party lines which have unhappily divided us, and to present an unbroken front in the preservation and defense of our interest." For a complete list of the resolutions, see Brown, *Baltimore and the 19th of April*, 37–38.

13. Maguire was getting a firsthand account from the witnesses of the Pratt Street riot. On April 19, 1861, the first group of volunteer Federal forces passed through Baltimore en route to protect the Union capital at Washington, DC. They arrived by the Northern Central Railroad in the northern part of the city. The Union forces consisted of the Sixth Massachusetts and seven companies of unarmed Pennsylvania volunteers. When the train of thirty-five cars carrying the troops arrived at the President Street Station, about nine cars containing seven companies of the Massachusetts Sixth reached the connecting station unmolested, suffering only jeers and hisses from the crowd. The next car was thrown off track and pelted by stones and other missiles. The succeeding cars were less fortunate. As the fury of the mob escalated, a cart coming by with a load of sand was dumped across the rail tracks. A pile of cobblestones slated for street repair was relocated to the improvised barricade. Large anchors from the wharf were dragged into the makeshift blockade, preventing further passage by rail cars. The obstructed cars reversed their track and returned to the President Street Station. The cars that were turned back contained four companies, C, D, I, and L, under Captains Follansbee, Hart, Pickering, and Dike. These companies formed on President Street amidst a dense and angry crowd and proceeded to march across the city

to the connecting station. During this march, shots were fired, resulting in the first casualty of the war. For a detail account of the Pratt Street riot see both Brown, *Baltimore and the 19th of April*, 37–38, and Sheads and Toomey, *Baltimore during the Civil War*, 15.

14. Acting without orders from the commander of the Union Army, Gen. Benjamin F. Butler took control of Baltimore. On the evening of May 13, he arrived in the city by train with one thousand soldiers consisting of the Sixth Massachusetts Regiment and the Boston Light Artillery. His forces disembarked at the Camden Street Station and quickly occupied Federal Hill. Once situated he sent the following message to the commander of Fort McHenry: "I have taken possession of Baltimore. My troops are on Federal Hill, which I can hold with the aid of my artillery. If I am attacked tonight, please open upon Battle [Monument] Square," which was in the middle of the city. Sheads and Toomey, *Baltimore during the Civil War*, 30.

15. The Fifth Maryland Infantry Regiment was organized at Baltimore City, Maryland, on September 12, 1861, to serve three years. Salome Marsh enlisted on September 24, 1861, under the rank of First Lieutenant Company B. The Regiment was attached to Dix's Division, Baltimore, Maryland, until March 1862. Early in the war the Fifth Regiment Infantry occupied a camp at Lafayette Square, Baltimore City, from September 1861 until March 1862, where they were drilled, disciplined, and prepared for active service in the field. Dyer, *A Compendium of the War of the Rebellion*, 1235.

16. Maguire and the Fifth Maryland were being mobilized as part of the Peninsula Campaign. This plan was devised by General McClellan and centered on moving against Richmond by way of the Chesapeake Bay. McClellan would move the army down the Chesapeake Bay to the southern tip of the Virginia Peninsula and then march them northward to Richmond. McClellan argued that this movement would take advantage of Federal sea power already in place just off the Virginia peninsula and put the army just fifty miles from Richmond. One long march would cut off the enemy forces holding the lower Virginia Peninsula between the York and the James; then two more days' march up the Peninsula would bring the army to the gates of Richmond. Strategically, this maneuver would also turn the flank of the Rebel army entrenched at Manassas forcing it to give up its position threatening Washington. The Confederate Army would have no choice but to defend the Confederate capital, leaving Washington behind. The idea was to force the enemy to move into a new position, while preventing it from reinforcing Confederate forces at Richmond. Federal forces in Tennessee would destroy the South's main east–west rail line and rail connections with the South Atlantic states to prevent Confederate reinforcements from arriving by rail. In the meantime, General McClellan would arrive at Richmond ahead of the Confederate commander and execute a battle on his own terms. Stephen W. Sears, *To*

the Gates of Richmond: The Peninsula Campaign (New York: Ticknor & Fields, 1992), 5–6. For more on the Peninsula Campaign see Gary W. Gallagher, The Richmond Campaign of 1862: The Peninsula and the Seven Days (Chapel Hill: University of North Carolina Press, 2000); David Glenn Brasher, The Peninsula Campaign and the Necessity of Emancipation: African Americans and the Fight for Freedoms (Chapel Hill: University of North Carolina Press, 2012); Kevin Dougherty and Michael Moore, The Peninsula Campaign of 1862: A Military Analysis (Jackson: University Press of Mississippi, 2010); Clifford Dowdy, The Seven Days: The Emergence of Lee (Boston, MA: Little, Brown, 1974); Angus Konstam, Fair Oaks 1862: McClellan's Peninsula Campaign (Westport, CT: Praeger, 2004); William J. Miller, ed., The Peninsula Campaign of 1862: Yorktown to the Seven Days (Boston, MA: De Capo Press, 1995), vol. 2; Rudolph J Schroeder III, Seven Days Before Richmond: McClellan's Peninsula Campaign of 1862 and its Aftermath (Bloomington, IN: iUniverse Press, 2009); Robert G. Tanner, Stonewall in the Valley: Thomas J. "Stonewall" Jackson's Shenandoah Valley Campaign, Spring 1862 (Garden City, NY: Doubleday, 1976).

17. The "Merrimac" that Maguire is referring to here was known as the ironclad. During this time period ship builders began to incorporate iron as covering for the hulls of war ships. The Gloire, built in France in 1857, was the first warship with an iron hull. Early in the war the Confederate Navy urged the Confederate Congress to fund the construction of an ironclad vessel. The first ironclad constructed was actually a conversion of an existing ship—the Merrimac. While the Confederacy rechristened her the Virginia, the Union continued to call her the Merrimac. The Confederacy had great hopes that this new ironclad vessel could destroy the Union blockading fleet and attack Washington, DC., from the Potomac. The Union responded by constructing three ironclad vessels of its own. Howard P. Nash, A Naval History of the Civil War (South Brunswick: A.S. Barnes, 1972), 79–83.

18. The Official War Record (OR) seems to contradict Maguire's account. According to the OR, the Fifth Maryland Infantry Regiment left Baltimore for the seat of war in Virginia at Fort Monroe on March 11, 1862, two days after the battle between the Monitor and the Merrimac. Upon arrival at Fort Monroe, they were assigned to General Dix's command in the Army of the Potomac and then to Weber's Brigade, Division at Suffolk, Va., 7th Army Corps, Dept. of Virginia, until September of 1862. Dyer, A Compendium of the War of Rebellion, 1235.

2. Summer on the Virginia Peninsula

1. Unknown to both the Union and Confederate commanders, the Confederate Navy chose the same weekend McClellan launched his Peninsula campaign to strike against the Federal blockade on the Virginia Peninsula. On Saturday March 8, the newly constructed Confederate ironclad

vessel—the CSS *Merrimac*—set sail from the shipyard at Norfolk and attacked the Union blockading squadron. The *Merrimac* destroyed two Union vessels and left Washington in a panic. The addition of an ironclad to the Confederate fleet posed a serious threat to the rest of the Union blockading force and the Union capital. This new development threatened to undo the plans for the Peninsular Campaign, but the Union Navy possessed an ironclad of its own, and as luck would have it, the Union ironclad USS *Monitor* arrived at Hampton Roads on the evening of Saturday, March 8. Before the *Monitor* arrived the *Merrimac* managed to scatter the Union fleet and sink two of the Union's most formidable vessels. Sears, *To the Gates of Richmond*, 19–29; Nash, *A Naval History of the Civil War*, 88–93.

2. The *Merrimac* set out from the Norfolk ship yard on the morning of March 8. Commanded by Franklin Buchanan, she headed straight for the Union ships blockading Norfolk. Among the Union fleet present were three sailing vessels and two steam frigates—the Congress, Cumberland, St. Lawrence, Roanoke and the Minnesota—all moored between Newport News and Fort Monroe. Nash, *A Naval History of the Civil War*, [88–93.]

3. The *Congress* was commanded by Lt. John L. Worden. The *Merrimac* was commanded by Franklin Buchanan. Buchanan's older brother, McKean, was the paymaster onboard the *Monitor*. During the engagement Franklin Buchanan was hit by a Minié ball while standing on top of the *Merrimac's* casement. McKean continued to serve the Union and rose in the navy ranks through the course of the war. Craig L. Symonds, *Confederate Admiral: The Life and Wars of Franklin Buchanan* (Annapolis, MD: Naval Institute Press, 1999), 47; Nash, *A Naval History of the Civil War*, 88–93.

4. The newly constructed *Monitor* commanded by Lt. John L. Worden left the Brooklyn New York ship yard for Hampton Roads on March 6. While the *Monitor* made its way down the northern Atlantic coast, it encountered rough weather conditions that tried the design of the new vessel and the endurance of her crew. She spent two days fighting a winter storm. The *Monitor* arrived in the Fort Monroe area around 4:00 p.m. on March 8. As she did so, her crew heard the booming of heavy guns as the *Merrimac* attempted to destroy the Union fleet. The following morning the *Monitor* surprised the crew of the *Merrimac* and proved herself a worthy opponent of the Confederate ironclad. Nash, *A Naval History of the Civil War*, 88–93.

5. After her first engagement with the *Monitor*, the *Merrimac* went back to Norfolk where she underwent extensive repair and received a new commander—Flag Officer Josiah Tattnall. The *Monitor* too changed command as the temporary command was relieved by William Jeffers. In early April General McClellan's host landed at Fort Monroe and began their march up the York Peninsula to Richmond. Three more times the *Merrimac* sortied down the Elizabeth River and challenged the *Monitor* to an-

other fight. But Jeffers, heeding orders, stayed safely under the guns of the Union shore batteries. Ivan Musicant, *Divided Waters: The Naval History of the Civil War* (New York: Harper Collins, 1995), 176. For more on naval history during the Civil War, see Michael J. Bennett, *Union Jacks, Yankee Sailors in the Civil War* (Chapel Hill: University of North Carolina Press, 2004); Saxton T. Bisbee, *Engines of Rebellion: Confederate Ironclads and Steam Engineering in the American Civil War* (Tuscaloosa: University of Alabama Press, 1986 and 2018); Paul Calore, *Naval Campaigns of the Civil War* (Jefferson, NC: McFarland, 2002); William M. Fowler, *Under Two Flags: The American Navy in the Civil War* (New York: Norton, 1990); Fuller J. Howard, *Clad in Iron: The American Civil War and the Challenge of British Naval Power* (Westport, CT: Praeger Security International, 2008); Anna Gibson Holloway and Jonathan W. White, *"Our Little Monitor": The Greatest Invention of the Civil War* (Kent, OH: Kent State University Press, 2018); James M. McPherson, *War on the Waters: The Union and Confederate Navies, 1861–1865* (Chapel Hill: University of North Carolina Press, 2012); David Porter, *The Naval History of the Civil War* (Secaucus, NJ: Castle, 1984); William H. Roberts, *Civil War Ironclads: The U.S. Navy and Industrial Mobilization*, paperback ed. (Baltimore, MD: Johns Hopkins University Press, 2007); Myron J Smith, *American Civil War Navies: A Bibliography.* (Metuchen, N.J: Scarecrow Press, 1972), vol. 3; Craig L. Symonds, *The Civil War at Sea* (Santa Barbara, CA: Praeger, 2009); Craig L. Symonds and Thomas B. Buell, *Decision at Sea: Five Naval Battles that Shaped American History* (New York and Oxford: Oxford University Press, 2005); Craig L. Symonds, *Union Combined Operations in the Civil War* (New York: Fordham University Press, 2010); Stephen R. Taaffe, *Commanding Lincoln's Navy: Union Naval Leadership during the Civil War* (Annapolis, MD: Naval Institute Press, 2009); United States Naval History Division, *Civil War Naval Chronology 1861–1865* (Washington, DC: G.P.O, 1971).

6. As the Army of the Potomac made its way up the Virginia peninsula the Confederacy abandoned Norfolk. On the morning of May 9, the Merrimac crew woke at mooring to find that Confederate flags no longer flew along the battlements. The Merrimac's size and draft made it impossible to move her up river to Richmond. Faced with no other alternative her commander ran her aground and set her on fire. In the early morning hours of May 11, she was blown to pieces when the fire ignited the magazines the crew had left on board. Nash, *A Naval History of the Civil War*, 97.

7. The Army of the Potomac was 70,000 men strong when it arrived on the Virginia Peninsula in March 1862. By April, 30,000 more had arrived bringing the total force to just over 100,000 men. James McPherson, *Ordeal by Fire: The Civil War and Reconstruction* (New York: Knopf, 1982), 258, and David Stephen Heidler, Jeanne T. Heidler, and David J. Coles, *Encyclopedia of the American Civil War: A Political, Social and Military History* (Santa Barbara, CA: ABC-CLIO, 2000), 1274.

8. For history on the soldier's daily life, see Bell Irvin Wiley, The Life of Johnny Reb: The Common Soldier of the Confederacy (Garden City, NY: Doubleday, 1943), and Bell Irvin Wiley, The Common Soldier in the Civil War (New York NY: Grosset & Dunlap, 1958); James M. McPherson, For Cause and Comrades: Why Men Fought in the Civil War (New York: Oxford University Press, 1997); Kathryn Shively Meir, Nature's Civil War: Common Soldiers and the Environment in 1862 Virginia (Chapel Hill: University of North Carolina Press, 2014); Reid Mitchell, Civil War Soldiers (New York: Viking, 1988); Jim Murphy, The Boys' War: Confederate and Union Soldiers Talk about the Civil War (New York: Clarion Books, 1990); Richard M. Reid, Freedom for Themselves: North Carolina's Black Soldiers in the Civil War Era (Chapel Hill: University of North Carolina Press, 1943 and 2008); James I. Robertson Jr., Soldiers Blue and Grey (Columbia: University of South Carolina Press, 1988).

9. Joseph King Fenno Mansfield was a civil engineer and a Union general in the American Civil War. He attended the US Military Academy and fought in the Mexican War. At the start of the Civil War, Mansfield commanded the Department of Washington from April 27 to August 17, 1861, and was promoted to brigadier general on May 6, 1861. He was also a brigade commander in the Department of Virginia from March to June 1862 and commanded the Suffolk Division of the VII Corps of the Department of Virginia in the vicinity of Suffolk until fall 1862. During the Battle of Antietam Mansfield was given command of the XII Corps of the Army of the Potomac where he was mortally wounded. John H. Eicher and David J. Eicher, Civil War High Commands (Stanford, CA: Stanford University Press, 2001), 363, 850; Stephen W. Sears, Landscape Turned Red: The Battle of Antietam (Boston, MA, and New York: Houghton Mifflin, 1983), 171–77.

10. In the Union armies, the design, arrangement, and number of uniform buttons often helped to distinguish rate, rating, and the branch of an officer or soldier. For example, field-grade officers typically wore two rows of buttons on their dress coats, while captains, lieutenants, and enlisted men had only a single row. Until the war of 1812 each regiment had its own buttons that were often similar in the case of like units, such as rifle and infantry regiments. By 1821, each arm had a button whose central design was an eagle with a shield. On the shield was a branch initial, with the most common letters A for artillery, C for cavalry, D for dragoons, and I for infantry. Bell Irvin Wiley, The Life of Billy Yank: The Common Soldier of the Union (Garden City, NY: Doubleday, 1971), 60; William K. Emerson, Encyclopedia of United States Army Insignia and Uniforms (Norman: University of Oklahoma Press, 1996), 59–61.

11. According to the official record, Salome Marsh entered the service as First Lieutenant, Company B, on September 24, 1861. He was promoted to captain, Company F, July 23, 1862; major, June 15, 1863; and then to lieutenant-colonel, May 12, 1864. History and Roster of Maryland Volunteers, War of 1861-6, vol. 1: 179–80.

12. From the mid-nineteenth century through World War I, Turner societies were among the most important secular organizations in German immigrant communities in America. Brought to the United States by refugees from the failed Revolution of 1848 in Germany, the Turner movement became a home for German abolitionists, workers' rights advocates, and other reformers. The societies were major centers of social, cultural, and athletic activities, particularly in the cities of the East and Midwest, and so played an important role in maintaining German culture while helping immigrants to adapt to American society. Eric Pumroy and Katja Rampelmann, *Research Guide to the Turner Movement in the United States* (Bibliographies and indexes in American history, no. 33. Westport, CT: Greenwood Press, 1996), 1–20.

13. The Sibley tent was a bell-shaped structure supported by a center pole that rested on a tripod. It was equipped with a stove the pipe of which passed through an opening at the apex. It could comfortably accommodate about a dozen men, but the army frequently crowded in more. Inhabitants arranged themselves for sleeping in the formation of wheel spokes, with feet at the center and heads near the circumference. Wiley, *The Life of Billy Yank*, 55–58.

14. Salome Marsh had married Margaret L. Maguire on June 2, 1850, at Baltimore City, Maryland. Baltimore County Court Marriage Licenses, 1846–1851 C376, at the Maryland Public Archives.

15. This was most likely the Hampton Hospital that was situated between Hampton Creek and Mill Creek, two miles from Fort Monroe, Virginia, on a nearly level plain, ten feet above and nearly surrounded by tide-water. It was opened in August 1862. Joseph K. Barnes, *The Medical and Surgical History of the Civil War* (Wilmington, NC: Broadfoot, 1990), vol. 11: 939.

16. Before the Civil War there were no trained nurses in the army and very few in the civilian world. Throughout the nineteenth century, nursing was done in the home, primarily by wives, daughters, and sisters. In the early campaigns of the war, soldiers suffered horribly due to a lack of nursing. Injured or sick soldiers often nursed each other with little or no training and as their conditions improved they were immediately sent back into battle. In addition to injuries sustained in battle, epidemics and diseases often ran rampant through both armies. By the end of 1862, the public was well aware of the deficiencies in military medical care, rallying hundreds of women to the cause on both sides. For the Union, women such as Clara Barton, Dorthea Dix, and Mother Bickerdyke began to lay the foundation for nursing as we know it today. The Civil War played a major role in the evolution of nursing in the United States. Alfred J. Bollet, *Civil War Medicine Challenges and Triumphs* (Tucson, AZ: Galen Press, LTD, 2002), 31, 132.

17. At the start of the Peninsula Campaign, the Army of the Potomac engaged in the siege of Yorktown, which allowed a Confederate Army of only

17,000 to delay its advance for a month. This gave the Confederate command time to interpose the bulk of the Confederate forces between the Army of the Potomac and Richmond. General McClellan greatly exaggerated the numbers of the opposition, believing them to be stronger than they actually were. McClellan made it to the Chickahominy River just five miles from Richmond. He arrived with five corps, positioning three north of the river, and two south of the river, unaware that his reinforcement would not be arriving. On May 31, the Confederate Commander, Joseph E. Johnston, threw the bulk of his forces against the two Union corps south of the Chickahominy in the battle of Seven Pines or Fair Oaks. McClellan was able to bring reinforcements from north of the river and halt the Confederate advance. Late in the afternoon Johnston was wounded, and President Davis named Robert E. Lee to command the army. Lee quickly decided to renew the attack against McClellan's forces concentrating on those that remained north of the river. Meanwhile McClellan held the rest of his army idle south of the Chickahominy. Unable to receive reinforcements due to the strategic accomplishments of the Confederate commanders, McClellan withdrew to Harrison's Landing on the James River, bringing the Peninsula Campaign to a close. Sears, *To the Gates of Richmond*.

18. McClellan's army of 90,000 was withdrawn to Harrison's Landing during which time his army was beginning to be crippled with sickness. President Lincoln and the newly appointed general and chief of all armies, Henry Halleck, decided to withdraw the Army of the Potomac from the Peninsula and send it by water to reinforce Gen. John Pope for the second battle at Manassas. McPherson, *Ordeal by Fire*, 266–77.

19. For more on the experiences of African Americans in the Civil War, see John David Smith, ed., *Black Soldiers in Blue: African American Troops in the Civil War Era* (Chapel Hill: University of North Carolina Press, 2002); James M. McPherson, *Marching Toward Freedom: The Negro in the Civil War* (New York: Knopf, 1967); Thavolia Glymph, "Noncombatant Military Laborers in the Civil War" in OAH *Magazine of History* 26, no. 2 (2012): 25–29; James M. McPherson, *The Negro's Civil War: How American Negroes Felt and Acted during the War for the Union* (New York: Pantheon Books, 1965); and David Herbert, ed., *Gone for a Soldier: the Civil War Memoirs of Private Alfred Bellard; from the Alec Thomas Archives* (Boston, MA: Little, Brown, 1975).

20. On May 20, 1861, the Vermont 1st Infantry demonstrated on Hampton Roads. On May 29, 1861 Hampton Roads was occupied by the New York 1st and 2nd Infantry. In the fall of 1861 Confederate Gen. Magruder burned the village of Hampton to the ground after newspapers announced that the Yankees were to convert the town to a settlement for runaway slaves. Sears, *To the Gates of Richmond*, 28.

21. The term Octoroon is defined as a person of one-eighth black ancestry.

22. Canister or grapeshot was the ammunition used in the six-pounder smoothbore cannon. This type of cannon was highly mobile and when

loaded with a hollow shell packed with lead balls and gun powder or a canister that was essentially a very large shotgun shell it was highly effective against infantry at short distances. Herman Hattaway, *Shades of Blue and Grey* (Columbia: University of Missouri Press, 1991), 40.

23. It is probable that the New York 1st and 2nd infantry left behind the comfortable camp complete with gymnasium that Maguire describes. These regiments fought at Big Bethel, Virginia, and shared duty at Camp Hamilton and Newport News until being joined to the Army of the Potomac. They witnessed the battle between the *Monitor* and *Merrimac* from Hampton Roads on March 8, 1862. Just before the Maryland 5th was moved from Newport News and attached to Weber's Brigade, Third Division, at Suffolk. The New York 1st and 2nd Infantry were sent to action near Fair Oaks on June 20, 23, and 24, Oak Grove on June 25, and the Seven Days battle from June 25 to July 1. Meanwhile, the Maryland 5th occupied the comfortable camp they left behind. Dyer, *A Compendium of the War of Rebellion*, 1367, 1372; Sears, *To the Gates of Richmond*, 28.

24. Following the withdrawal of the Army of the Potomac to Harrison's Landing, McClellan was relieved of field command. Gen. John Pope replaced him and led the army into the Second Battle of Bull Run. The Union forces were severely beaten and retreated back to Washington. General McClellan was reinstated as commander of the Army of Potomac. In spite of his problems in the field, McClellan had proven himself an unparalleled organizer, capable of shaping and unifying the Army of the Potomac back into a fighting machine. By September of 1862 they were ready to pursue and engage the invading Confederate forces led by Robert E. Lee at the Battle of Antietam. John Cannan, *The Antietam Campaign August-September 1862* (Conshohocken, PA: Combined Books, 1994), 236.

3. Into Battle at Antietam

1. In September of 1862 the Maryland 5th was moved to Washington, DC, and thence to Antietam. The Maryland 5th was added to the new larger Army of the Potomac in Edward Sumner's Second Corps, Third Division, commanded by Gen. William H. French, Third Brigade commanded by Brig. Gen. Max Weber. Dyer, *A Compendium of the War of Rebellion*, 1235; Cannan, *The Antietam Campaign*, 236.

2. For more on the experiences and motivations of Civil War soldiers, see Michael Barton, *Good Men: The Character of Civil War Soldiers* (University Park: Pennsylvania State University Press, 1981); Michael Barton and Larry M. Logue, eds., *The Civil War Soldier: A Historical Reader* (New York: New York University Press, 2002); Peter S. Carmichael, *The War for the Common Soldier: How Men Thought, Fought, and Survived in Civil War Armies* (Chapel Hill: University of North Carolina Press, 2018); Joseph T. Glatthaar, *The March to the Sea and Beyond: Sherman's troop in the Savannah and Carolinas Campaigns*

(Baton Rouge,: Louisiana State University Press, 1995); Earl J. Hess, *The Union Soldier in Battle Enduring the Ordeal of Combat* (Lawrence: University Press of Kansas, 1997); Earl J. Hess, *Liberty, Virtue, and Progress: Northerners and Their War for the Union* (New York: New York University Press, 1988); Gerald F. Linderman, *Embattled Courage: The Experience of Combat in the American Civil War* (New York and London: Free Press, 1987).

3. By September 13, 1862, the Army of the Potomac was concentrated around Fredrick. Roland, *An American Iliad*, 78–84.

4. On September 4, 1862, the Confederate Army of Northern Virginia crossed the Potomac forty miles upriver from Washington. Once past Frederick, Maryland, Lee divided his army into five separate parts. Three separate columns were ordered to converge on Harpers Ferry. Two divisions were sent to Hagerstown, and another division at Boonsboro, near Turners Gap, where the National Road crossed South Mountain. The Army of the Potomac marched from Washington to Frederick between September 3 and 13. When they arrived at Frederick, McClellan and the bulk of his army made camp only twelve miles from the nearest Confederate units. Among the first units to arrive was the First Division of the Twelfth Corps. One of the regiments, the 27th Indiana set up camp on the outskirts of town when Sgt. John M. Bloss and Corp. Barton W. Mitchell of Company F noticed a bulky envelope in the tall grass nearby. Inside was a sheet of paper wrapped around three cigars titled "Headquarters, Army of Northern Virginia, Special Orders, No. 191, September 9" The find was sent to General McClellan arming him with the Confederates' plan. He knew where they were and what they were planning. Sears, *Landscape Turned Red*, 112–13.

5. Stonewall Jackson's vanguard arrived at Frederick September 6, 1862. Stephen W. Sears argues that in the annals of American literature, the singular consequence of the Confederate occupation of Frederick was the inspiration it furnished the poet John Greenleaf Whittier, whose "Barbara Fritchie" swelled patriotic spirits across the North when it appeared in the *Atlantic* in 1863. Legend has it that ninety-six-year-old Mrs. Fritchie reputedly defied the Confederate troops under Stonewall Jackson as they advanced through Frederick, Maryland, by waving the Stars and Stripes from an upper window of her home. Sears contends that at the time no one made note of any rifle blast unleashed by a rebel horde at any national flag, particularly one held by an elderly woman out a window. The evidence reveals that a ninety-six-year-old Mrs. Fritchie did live in Frederick, and she did wave a flag from her porch when Union troops arrived. A Mrs. Mary Quatrel was also seen to wave the stars and stripes at a passing Confederate column. The legend to emerge was disputed by Jackson's staff and the *Richmond Examiner*. In spite of this, Barbara Fritchie was considered a national heroine, and the poem entitled *Shame*—written on her behalf by Whittier—remains a national treasure. Sears, *Landscape Turned Red*, 93.

6. Maguire was most likely in Middletown, about eight miles from Frederick, when his brother-in-law tried to send him home.
7. For insight to the experiences of other Marylanders, see Kathleen Ernst, *Too Afraid to Cry: Maryland Civilians in the Antietam Campaign* (Mechanicsburg, PA: Stackpole Books, 1999).
8. With the Army of the Potomac now between Washington and the Confederates, Lee took a strategic gamble. He had anticipated that Harpers Ferry would be evacuated. When he found that it was not, he divided his army, sending Maj. Gen. Andrew Jackson, Maj. Gen. Lafayette McLaws, and Brig. Gen. John G. Walker to capture Harpers Ferry, while his own force proceeded toward Hagerstown. Once Harpers Ferry was captured, the three corps would unite with the main bulk of the army in the west-central part of the state. To accomplish this, Lee was relying on McClellan's reputation of hesitating and acting slowly, giving the Confederate forces time enough to strike and reunite. McClellan was armed with the Confederate plan, and it soon became apparent to Lee that McClellan was anticipating his moves. McClellan moved quicker than expected on the heels of the Confederate forces, but not quick enough to prevent Lee from establishing lines of defenses at the base of South Mountain at Turners Gap and Crampton's Gap to prevent the Army of the Potomac from advancing any further. These efforts failed, as the Confederate forces were outnumbered, and outmaneuvered by the Union corps sent to break through on September 14, 1863. The Confederate forces retreated from both gaps, clearing the way to Hagerstown for the Union forces. The fighting was fierce. The total losses for the Federals in the fight for Crampton's Gap totaled 531. It is estimated that the Confederate losses were about the same with an additional 400 taken prisoner. In the struggle for Turners Gap, the Federals lost just over 1,800 men. It is estimated that the Confederates lost 2,300. Sears, *Landscape Turned Red*, 142–46. For an excellent account of the Battle of South Mountain, see Brian Matthew Jordan, *Unholy Sabbath: The Battle of South Mountain in History and Memory: September 14, 1862* (New York: Savas Beatie, 2012). For more on Lee and McClellan see Douglas S. Freeman, *R. E. Lee: A Biography* (New York, London: C. Scribner's Sons, 1934); Joseph Harsh, *Confederate Tide Rising: Robert E. Lee and the Making of Southern Strategy, 1961–1862* (Kent, OH: Kent State University Press, 1998); Joseph H Harsh, *Taken at the Flood: Robert E. Lee and Confederate strategy in the Maryland campaign of 1862* (Kent, OH: Kent State University Press, 1998); Warren W. Hassler, *General George B. McClellan: Shield of the Union* (Baton Rouge: Louisiana State University Press, 1957); Ethan Rafuse, *McClellan's' War: The Failure of Moderation in the Struggle for the Union* (Bloomington: Indiana University Press, 2005); and Stephen Sears, *George B. McClellan: The Young Napoleon* (New York: Ticknor & Fields, 1988).
9. After the Confederate forces withdrew from Crampton's and Turners Gap, the survivors and some fresh troops formed a battle line across Pleasant

Valley in between South Mountain and Hagerstown. On the brink of withdrawal, the tide changed for the Confederacy with the successful capture of Harpers Ferry. General Lee decided to stay put and give battle on northern soil. On September 15 the Army of the Potomac advanced towards Hagerstown. By early afternoon the Fifth Maryland, as part of the Second Corps commanded by Maj. Gen. Edwin Sumner, had passed through Boonsboro and were two miles beyond the village of Keedysville. They halted along the turnpike from Boonsboro to Sharpsburg, just behind Antietam Creek. On the far side of Antietam Creek, the Confederate Army waited in a line of battle and sharpshooters fired at anyone they thought they could hit. The two armies faced one another, and, as they did so, the batteries of both sides commenced a long-range duel. Sears, *Landscape Turned Red*, 159–65.

10. On September 16, the Union forces spent the day idle at camp. As they did, Jackson rejoined Lee's forces. This day was originally planned as the day of battle, but it brought only sporadic shelling, as thousands in both armies steeled themselves for the combat to come. McClellan was not ready. In spite of this, Maj. Gen. Joseph Hooker led the I Corps from its camp at Keedysville across the upper bridge over Antietam Creek to Hagerstown Pike. They ran into a strong Confederate picket line towards dusk. The fighting was inconclusive and died off in the darkness. This is thought by some to have been the beginning of the Battle of Antietam. Sears, *Landscape Turned Red*, 162–65; David Donald, Jean Harvey Baker, and Michael F. Holt, *The Civil War and Reconstruction* (New York and London: Norton), 218–19; Cannan, *The Antietam Campaign*, 131.

11. McClellan attacked the Confederate forces at dawn on September 17, 1862. He organized the Union forces into six corps and a cavalry division. Maguire and the Fifth Maryland were attached to the II Corps, commanded by Maj. Gen. Edwin V. Sumner. They were assigned directly under Brig. Gen. William H. French as part of the third brigade, commanded by Gen. Max Weber. At dawn on September 17, 1862, the II Corps was bivouacked near McClellan's headquarters at the Pry house, just east of the Antietam Creek, and just under two miles directly east of where Hooker opened the battle at Dunkers Church. Sears, *Landscape Turned Red*, 195.

12. Dr. William H. Norris enlisted in the Fifth Maryland at Baltimore on October 2, 1861. His initial enlistment was as an assistant surgeon. He mustered out on August 8, 1862—this may have been a result of being reassigned to Pope's command on the Rapidan River when Lincoln began withdrawing McClellan's army from the Peninsula. Dr. Norris was then mustered back in as a surgeon on September 3, 1862. He remained an officer of the Fifth Maryland Regiment until October 1, 1864. *History and Roster of Maryland Volunteers, War of 1861–6* vol. 1: 181.

13. At 7:20 Maguire and the Fifth Maryland marched into battle with the

Second Corps as part of Brig. Gen. William H. French's division. They crossed Antietam Creek at a ford just below the northern bridge, marched up the slopes of the creek bank, across the open pasture that separated the Roulette and Mumma farms, and arrived at the edge of the East Woods. When French's division reached the East Woods, the rest of the Corps was out of sight, having been left behind. French decided to move his forces southward. However, Maguire's descriptions of entering the battlefield field also resemble the experiences of the Second Division led by Maj. Gen. John Sedgwick. When Sedgwick reached the East Woods, he continued due west through the cornfield, over the fences along the Hagerstown Turnpike and into the West Woods. Sears, *Landscape Turned Red*, 222–39.

14. French advanced his men across the Mumma cornfield, and through the pasture and apple orchard of the Roulette farm. The brigade brushed aside a small Confederate outpost along the way and moved steadily south. They climbed the north face of a long limestone ridge. When they reached the crest and looked down below them they saw a sunken lane packed with armed Confederates. This sunken lane would become the famous Bloody Lane. McPherson, *Ordeal by Fire*, 306; Cannan, *The Antietam Campaign*, 159–67; Sears, *Landscape Turned Red*, 237; Antietam National Battlefield Archives; Gary Gallagher, *The Antietam Campaign: Military Campaigns of the Civil War* (Chapel Hill: University of North Carolina Press, 1999), 231.

15. Maguire may have found himself at an irrigation canal for the Mumma or Poffenberger farmhouse.

16. As the Fifth Maryland came through the Mumma cornfield and approached the crest of the ridgeline that ran along the Sunken Road, they were ordered to charge. Within five minutes their brigade suffered 450 casualties. The fight at the Bloody Lane went on for more than two hours. For the Fifth Maryland, 550 men were present, 25 were killed, 123 wounded, and 15 missing, for a total of 163. McPherson, *Ordeal by Fire*, 306; Cannan, *The Antietam Campaign*, 159–67; Sears, *Landscape Turned Red*, 238; Antietam National Battlefield Archives; Gallagher, *The Antietam Campaign*, 231.

17. As French's division moved across the Roulette farm, rebel skirmishers were chased out of the Roulette buildings and the regiment surgeons took over the Roulette barn, converting it into a field hospital. Meanwhile, to the north the regiment surgeons from the First Corps set up a field hospital at the Poffenberger farm. If Maguire did in fact end up with Sedgwick's division, then the time he spent in a field hospital for the remainder of the battle was at the Poffenberger farmhouse. Sears, *Landscape Turned Red*, 237, 306.

18. After the first battle of the war it was clear that the Army Medical Department was wholly unprepared and disorganized. In addition to being

understaffed, the Union Army lacked the resources for erecting adequate
field hospitals and moving the wounded off the field. There was no artic-
ulated organization, and medical directors out in the field had no guid-
ance or operating procedures to get things done. In the spring of 1862 the
secretary of war removed the surgeon general and replaced him with a
young physician, William A. Hammond. Hammond implemented new
examination boards for field surgeons, reorganized the medical personnel in the field, and together with General McClellan created an ambulance corps and graded system to move the wounded off the field. These
innovations, combined with the efforts of civilian volunteers, helped to
improve the care provided in the field, although as Maguire's narrative
reveals there were many obstacles to overcome. Alfred J. Bollett, M.D.,
Civil War Medicine (Tucson, AZ: Galen Press, 2002), 19, 32.

19. During this time period doctors often disagreed on the merits of amputation. Many placed a priority on saving injured limbs, and others believed
that amputation was the best way to save lives. The procedures of the
time often resulted in infection that could be fatal to the patient. In a
war environment, patients were routinely malnourished, roughly handled during transportation, and exposed to unsanitary conditions that
favored amputation. George Worthington Adams, *Doctors in Blue: the Medical History of the Union Army in the Civil War* (New York: H. Schuman, 1952),
116–18.

20. When it was clear that the Confederate Army would give fight at Antietam, Clara Barton was determined to be on the scene before the fighting began. From her warehouse command post in Washington, DC, she
collected supplies and arranged items for the field. She set out towards
Harpers Ferry on September 14, and made it safely to Frederick, but the
Confederates had wrecked the railroad bridge across the Monocacy River,
causing a massive traffic jam of supply trains. Among the jammed supply
train were the very trains commissioned by the Army Medical Director
to carry medical supplies to the battlefield. Abandoning hope of getting
to Harpers Ferry, Barton took a road off the Boonsboro Pike that crossed
the Potomac at the upper bridge near Pry's Mill Ford. She arrived at a
hospital in the cornfield just west of the East Woods at the Poffenberger
Farm, where she worked for three days straight before succumbing to
typhoid fever. She was taken back to Washington, DC. Stephen Oates,
A Woman of Valor: Clara Barton and the Civil War (New York: Free Press,
1994), 77–93. For more on Clara Barton, see Blanche Colton Williams,
Clara Barton, Daughter of Destiny (Philadelphia and New York: J.B. Lippincott Company, 1941); Ishbell Ross, *Angel of the Battlefield: The Life of Clara
Barton* (New York: Harper, 1956); and Donald C. Pfanz, *Clara Barton's Civil
War: Between Bullet and Hospital* (Yardley, PA: Westholme, 2018). For more
on nurses, see John R. Brumgardt, *Civil War Nurse: The Diary and Letters of*

Hannah Ropes (Knoxville: University of Tennessee Press, 1993); Richard B. Harwell, *Kate: The Journal of a Confederate Nurse* (Baton Rouge: Louisiana State University Press, 1959); and Ann Douglas Wood, "The War Within a War: Women Nurses in the Union Army," *Civil War History* 18 (3) (1972).

21. The regiment fought bravely and suffered severely in killed and wounded at the Bloody Lane. The commanding officer, Maj. Leopold Blumenberg, was seriously wounded at the head of the regiment and was carried to the rear. Capt. W. W. Bamberger of Company B then assumed command of the regiment. In turn, he was seriously wounded and taken to the rear. At this point the command of the regiment went to Maguire's brother-in-law, Capt. Salome Marsh of Company F, who commanded the regiment for the rest of the day. There are two monuments to the regiment at Antietam, both near the Sunken Road (Bloody Lane) off Richardson Avenue. The main monument is on the north side of the Sunken Lane about 225 feet east of where it splits off from Richardson Avenue. It was dedicated on September 17, 1890. A monument to the Regiment's Companies A and I is a short distance to the north from the main monument. It was dedicated on May 30, 1900.

22. General McClellan established his headquarters at the Pry House, on the high ground just east of Antietam Creek. Cannan, *The Antietam Campaign*, 118.

23. Antietam Creek had four bridges. One of which was on the Sharpsburg and Rohrersville Road, known as the Rohrbach Bridge. While the Fifth Maryland and the rest of French's unit attacked the Confederates at the Bloody Lane, Commander Maj. Gen. Ambrose E. Burnside and Brig. Gen. Jacob D. Cox of the Ninth Corps were ordered to attack on the Rohrbach Bridge. The Rohrbach Bridge was a triple-arch stone span 125 feet long and a dozen feet wide. It was one of the most defensible spots on the battlefield. The valley of the Antietam is narrow here, flanked on both sides by steep hills. The Confederates could not have asked for better terrain to defend. The wooded heights of the creek slanted steeply to the water's edge, and on the hillside overlooking the bridge was a stone wall and a quarry that had been further strengthen by the rebels with fence posts and fallen timber. On higher ground to the rear there were three batteries with a dozen guns for close support, and on a plateau in front of Sharpsburg were two more batteries whose guns commanded the bridge. The one positive for Burnside and Cox's forces was that the Confederates possessed too few infantrymen to hold it. When the initial attacks failed, Cox and Burnside decided to charge straight down the hill facing the bridge. They had 300 yards of open ground to cross and, as the Union forces did so, the Confederates hit them hard. After the firefight had gone on for some minutes, the Confederate resistance began to run out of ammunition and withdrew. By one o'clock, General Burnside had

captured the bridge. Sears, *Landscape Turned Red*, 256–66. For more on the battle of Antietam: Dennis E. Frye, *Antietam Revealed: The Battle of Antietam and the Maryland Campaign as You Have Never Seen It Before* (Collingwood, NJ: C.W. Historicals, 2004); Gary W. Gallagher, ed., *Antietam: Essays on the 1862 Maryland Campaign* (Kent, OH: Kent State University Press, 1989); D. Scott Hartwig, *To Antietam Creek: The Maryland Campaign of September 1862* (Baltimore, MD: Johns Hopkins University Press, 2012); James Murfin, *The Gleam of Bayonets: The Battle of Antietam and the Maryland Campaign of 1862* (Baton Rouge: Louisiana State University Press, 1982); Francis Palfrey, *The Antietam and Fredericksburg* (New York: Charles Scribner's Sons, 1882).

24. For more on civil war medicine, see Compiled by the U.S. War Department, Office of the Surgeon General, *The Medical and Surgical History of the War of Rebellion*, 6 vols. (1875–1888); Horace H. Cunningham, *Doctors in Grey* (Baton Rouge: Louisiana State University Press, 1959); Robert E. Denney, *Civil War Medicine* (New York: Sterling Publishers, 1994); Frank R. Freemon, *Microbes and Minie Balls: An Annotated Bibliography of Civil War Medicine* (Rutherford: Fairleigh Dickinson University Press, 1993); and Frank R. Freemon, *Gangrene and Glory: Medical Care during the Civil War* (Rutherford: Fairleigh Dickinson University Press, 1999).

25. The September 23, 1862, edition of the *Baltimore Sun* provides a complete list of casualties from the Fifth Maryland Regiment, including such detail as the nature and severity of their injuries. *Baltimore Sun* Historical Archives.

26. Following the Battle of Antietam, the Fifth Maryland Regiment did a reconnaissance mission to Charleston Harbor on October 16–17, 1862. They then moved to Harpers Ferry on September 22, 1862, and stayed until January of 1863. Dyer, *A Compendium of the War of Rebellion*, 1235.

4. Union Occupation of Harpers Ferry, 1862–1863

1. The town of Harpers Ferry was fifty miles from Washington, in Jefferson County, West Virginia. The town was situated on a narrow angle of land where the Shenandoah River enters the Potomac and is dominated by high ground on every side. To the north towered Maryland Heights, to the west Bolivar Heights, and to the south and east Loudoun Heights. With a natural strategic advantage, the home to weapon manufacturers, ammunition depots and a thoroughfare for the Baltimore and Ohio Railroad, Harpers Ferry was a very important place. It was captured by Confederate forces on September 15, 1862, but they had no intention of holding it. Instead, the Confederates stripped it of Union supplies, destroyed the pontoon bridge over the Potomac and the locks of the Chesapeake and Ohio canal, and evacuated it by September 20. The Union Quarter Master General Montgomery C. Meigs wanted Harpers Ferry reoccupied as soon as possible so that supplies could be sent by railroad and the ca-

nal. On September 22, McClellan ordered Burnside to reoccupy Harpers Ferry and reorganize the town's defenses. The pontoon bridge was ordered rebuilt and the canal locks were fixed. By September 24, nine days after the Union surrender, the Army of the Potomac occupied Harpers Ferry once again. Chester G. Hearn, *Six Years of Hell: Harpers Ferry during the Civil War* (Baton Rouge: Louisiana State University Press, 1996), 190–92. For more on Harpers Ferry, see Dennis E. Frye, *Harpers Ferry Under, Fire A Border Town in the American Civil War* (Brookfield, MO: Donning Company Publishers, 2011); D. E. Frye, *Harpers Ferry Nestled Between North and South* (Harrisburg, PA: Weider History Group, 2008); Ray Jones, *Harpers Ferry* (Gretna, LA: Pelican, 1992) and Ethan S. Rafuse, *Antietam, South Mountain, and Harpers Ferry* (Lincoln: University of Nebraska Press, 2008).

2. John Brown was an American abolitionist who attempted to end slavery by force of arms. Born on May 9, 1800, in Connecticut, he became famous after orchestrating and leading two violent clashes in the name of abolitionism. The first was in Lawrence, Kansas, on May 24, 1856, when he and three of his sons avenged the deaths of fellow abolitionists by killing five proslavery supporters. The second was on October 16, 1859, when Brown and a force of eighteen men seized the arsenal at Harpers Ferry in an attempt to free the slaves of Virginia by force of arms. Ill-planned and ill-orchestrated, the attempt was squashed by local militia and a company of United States Marines commanded by US Col. Robert E. Lee. Brown went on to stand trial and was hanged on December 2, 1859, at Charles Town, Virginia. Many historians credit John Brown's violent clash at Harpers Ferry as the spark that ignited the Civil War. Hearn, *Six Years of Hell*, 10–30. For more on John Brown, see Jules Abels, *Man on Fire: John Brown and the Cause of Liberty* (New York: Macmillan, 1971); Benjamin Franklin Cooling III, *Counter-Thrust: From the Peninsula to the Antietam* (Lincoln: University of Nebraska Press, 2007); and Jonathan Earle, *John Brown's Raid on Harpers Ferry: A Brief History with Documents* (Boston: Bedford/St. Martin's, 2008).

3. In January of 1863 the Fifth Maryland was ordered to Point of Rocks for the defenses of the Baltimore and Ohio Railroad. Dyer, *A Compendium of the War of Rebellion*, 1235.

4. William S. Fish was provost marshall of Baltimore in 1863 but was arrested in 1864 on charges of fraud and corruption by the secretary of war. Fish and his associates would arrest innocent people and then come to their rescue for a price. Fish was found guilty and sent to prison in New York. Sheads and Toomey, *Baltimore during the Civil War*, 63.

5. For more information about Jews in the Civil War, see Bertram Wallace Korn, *American Jewry and the Civil War* (Philadelphia, PA: The Jewish Publication Society of America, 1951); Robert N. Rosen, *The Jewish Confederates* (Columbia: University of South Carolina Press, 2000); Harry Simonoff,

Jewish Participants in the Civil War (New York: Arco, 1963); Jonathan D. Sarna, *Jews and the Civil War: A Reader* (New York: New York University Press, 2010); and Jonathan D. Sarna, *Lincoln and the Jews: A History* (New York: Thomas Dunne Books/St. Martin's Press, 2015).

6. It is interesting to note that one of the cases that Provost Marshall Fish was prosecuted for involved a Jewish doctor named Dr. Friedenwald, who was arrested for running the blockade in 1863. Fish charged Friedenwald's family $50,000 for his release. Sheads and Toomey, *Baltimore during the Civil War*, 63.

7. Both the North and the South suffered tremendous deprivation from the inability to obtain adequate supplies for both the military and civilian populations. Inflation neared 700 percent as the economies on both sides of the Mason–Dixon line struggled. There was a great deal of hoarding and speculation among traders, many of whom were believed to be Jewish. The frustration inherent in combating price gouging, shortages, and waste resulted in the emergence of a form of anti-Semitism in both the North and the South. Maguire's mention of Jewish traders is significant when considered within this context. In December of 1862, Gen. Ulysses S. Grant and Gen. William Tecumseh Sherman attempted to suppress trade by Jewish traders by issuing an order to expel Jews from Tennessee, Kentucky, and Mississippi. This famous order, Order 11, was promptly rescinded by President Lincoln, and Grant later apologized, citing economic frustration as the instigator and not anti-Semitism, as many believed. The Confederate War Department also used Jewish traders as a scapegoat for waste and mismanagement of food and clothing. Donald, Baker, and Holt, *The Civil War and Reconstruction*, 52, 439, 458.

8. What Maguire refers to as the Cumberland Canal was most likely the Chesapeake and Ohio Canal. Called the C&O, this canal ran parallel to the Potomac River and passed through Harpers Ferry and Point of Rocks connecting Washington, DC, to Cumberland Maryland. The C&O Canal operated from 1836 until 1924, providing a transportation route primarily for coal from the Allegheny Mountains. For more on the C&O Canal, see Thomas F. Hahn, *The Chesapeake and Ohio Canal: Pathway to the Nation's Capital* (Metuchen, NJ: Scarecrow Press, 1984).

9. This was a heroic act for a boy of thirteen or fourteen.

10. *The War of the Rebellion: a Compilation of the Official Records of the Union and Confederate Armies* compiled by the United States War Department following the war details instances of corruption within Union ranks and general orders designed to prevent the taking of bribes by military personnel from civilians. Preventing extortion was a serious challenge for Union leaders. Understood within this historical context, it makes sense that Maguire's brother-in-law would have chosen him to issue passes. His young age and position within the regiment made him less susceptible to bribery. For an example of an executive order of this nature, see Robert N.

Scott, H. M. Lazelle, George Davis, Leslie J. Perry, Joseph W. Kirkley, Fred C. Ainsworth, John S. Moodey, Calvin D. Cowles, *The War of the Rebellion: A Compilation of the Official Records of the Union and Confederate Armies* (Washington: Government Printing Office, 1880), serial 025, chapter XXIX, 0158.

11. The Fifth Maryland remained on the Upper Potomac and in the Shenandoah Valley during the winter of 1863. On June 2, it was assigned to General Milroy's command and moved to Winchester, Virginia, where they engaged in the Battle of Winchester, June 13–15. Most of the regiment was captured. Dyer, *A Compendium of the War of Rebellion*, 1235.

12. Libby Prison was a Confederate prison located in Richmond, Virginia. The prison itself was a large three-story brick warehouse that had been used as a grocery store and ship's chandlery before the war. When the war began, the Confederacy commandeered the building for use as a prison. Throughout the course of the war, Libby Prison became notorious for the tremendous death rate among prisoners. After the war, the structure was dismantled, and relocated piece by piece by piece to Chicago where it was reassembled and made into a Civil War museum. In 1899 the structure was demolished and pieces of it were sold to collectors or thrown away. Heidler, Heidler, and Coles, *Encyclopedia of the American Civil War*, 1180. For more on Libby Prison, see Joseph Wheelan, *Libby Prison Breakout: The Daring Escape from the Notorious Civil War Prison* (New York: Public Affairs, 2010).

13. Salome Marsh was in command of his regiment when he was captured by General Ewell's Corps near Winchester on the Martinsburg Road. The first two weeks of his captivity was spent in a hospital due to ill health, after which he was sent to Libby Prison. In the first four months of his incarceration, he was fed half a loaf of bread, four ounces of meat, and a spoonful of rice per day. After four months the meat was removed and only provided occasionally. Eventually the bread stopped, and in its place prisoners were fed a coarse cornbread. After some months of this diet, Marsh grew sick and returned to the hospital. While at the hospital he saw some enlisted prisoners who appeared to be the starving victims of Confederate tactics of revenge unleashed upon Union prisoners. Marsh remained at Libby Prison from June 15, 1863, to March 21, 1864. For the full account of his experience while in Libby Prison, see Edward Steers, *The Trial: The Assassination of President Lincoln and the Trial of the Conspirators* (Lexington: University Press of Kentucky, 2003), 57–58.

5. Return to Baltimore: Hicks United States General Hospital

1. The guerilla Maguire is referring to may have been Maj. Harry W. Gilmore. Gilmore was a Baltimorean who joined the Confederate cavalry. Throughout the summer of 1864, Major Gilmore led a small cavalry unit in a series of raids around Baltimore for the purpose of disrupting communications

between large northern cities. Toomey, Daniel Carroll, "Gilmore's Raid," lecture, Jerusalem Mill Village, Kingsville, MD, July 11, 2009.

2. In addition to Gilmore's raids around Baltimore, the city's proximity to the battle at Antietam terrified Baltimoreans and propelled people to erect barricades and construct a series of camps, forts, and redoubts throughout the city for the city's defense. By the end of 1864, forty-two known fortified sites encircled Baltimore, guarding vital rail lines and places of encampment as regiments passed through during the war, or as regional military engagement prompted additional security measures. Sheads and Toomey, Baltimore during the Civil War, 123.

3. In 1861, the Union raised forty volunteer regiments for a term of two years. In the fall of 1862, ninety more regiments were called up for a term of nine months. By the spring of 1863, the number of volunteers began to diminish, and President Lincoln passed the Enrollment Act in an attempt to rally more. The Enrollment Act made every man age twenty to forty-five eligible for conscription and mandated each congressional district a quota based on a formula that factored in the number of available men minus the number of men who had or were currently, serving. With only fifty days to fill the quota, local officials offered cash bounties at the time of enlistment in an attempt to reduce the number of men who would have to be drafted. This system of bounties created many problems. The districts that could offer the highest bounties recruited the most volunteers. There were no restrictions on substitutes, and the price for substitutes often soared, in spite of a law permitting a drafted man to pay a three-hundred-dollar commutation fee to avoid that particular draft. Some men also resorted to "bounty jumping" by signing up in one district, collecting the bounty, and then signing up in another to collect the bounty again. However, the biggest problem was the resentment this system of bounties generated in volunteer soldiers. Volunteers often resented and shunned the soldiers who entered service through the bounty system. McPherson, Ordeal by Fire, 384–85.

4. When the war began the Union allowed boys under the age of eighteen to enlist with the permission of their parents. In 1862, the enlistment of boys under the age of eighteen was prohibited, but heavy casualties compelled recruiting officers to often overlook the age of a volunteer. As a result, thousands of boys enlisted in the Union Army. These boys acted as drummers, carrying messages between commands, and signaling reveille, company taps, and roll calls. They carried canteens to the sick and wounded and assisted surgeons in the field. Some also participated in the fighting. Steven Mintz, Huck's Raft: A History of American Childhood (Cambridge, MA: Belknap Press of Harvard University Press, 2004), 121.

5. The new hospitals being erected by the Army Medical Department were called "general" hospitals because the patients they accepted were not

limited by unit or post. Early in the war these hospitals were often inadequate, poorly constructed, or improvised within existing structures. In an attempt to correct this, the surgeon general created a hospital system that treated over a million soldiers with a mortality rate of only 8 percent. The new hospitals were designed as pavilion hospitals with long wings branching out from a central building on the theory that this would permit better segregation of the various categories of hospital cases and would inhibit the concentration of contagious air typical of older hospitals. Combined with the noted positive effects of fresh air discovered by Florence Nightingale, these innovations informed the construction of hospital pavilions, such as the one experienced by Maguire at Hick's. Hick's United States General Hospital was opened on June 9, 1865. It was erected on Townsend Street in a northwestern suburb of the city. The detail of its construction was overseen by Surgeon Thomas Sims. The original design planned a circular hospital with thirty-six radiating wards that could accommodate sixty patients each. As the war came to a close, however, the plans were revised, and it became a hospital of eighteen wards, in a semicircular plan projecting from a covered corridor. It was considered one of the best hospitals constructed during the war because of many innovations included in the design. Barnes, *The Medical and Surgical History of the Civil War*, vol. 6: 949.

6. The diagram Maguire provides is an accurate depiction of the layout of the architectural design. For a lithograph of Hicks United States General Hospital, see the Maryland Public Archives Image Title: Hicks U.S. Genl. Hospital, Baltimore, Md. / Wm. Q. Caldwell, Jun. architect ; lith. & print by E. Sachse & Co., Balto. CALL NUMBER: PGA —Sachse & Co. Hicks (D size) [P&P] REPRODUCTION NUMBER: LC-USZC2–3800 (color film copy slide)MEDIUM: 1 print : lithograph, color. CREATED/PUBLISHED: Pub. by Bar Kane, c1864.CREATOR: E. Sachse & Co., lithographer.

7. The administration building formed the front of the hospital and faced outward in the middle of the straight line bounding the semicircular area. It was 132 by 38 feet and two stories high. The first floor contained the offices of the surgeons in charge, the executive officer, quartermaster, and commissary, the hospital library, and printing office; the second floor contained the quarters of the medical officers. A covered pathway in the rear of these buildings connected the ends of the semicircular corridor to which the wards were attached. Barnes, *The Medical and Surgical History of the Civil War*, vol. 6: 949.

8. The wards were arranged along the convexity of the corridor, nine on each side of a central two-story building. They were built and ventilated in accordance with new innovative regulations issued by the War Department. By this time in the war a great deal had been learned about the importance of good ventilation. The bathrooms and water closets were at the

free extremity of each and were furnished with a small stove and boiler for the supply of hot water. The water closets contained troughs, which were emptied and flushed several times a day into well-conditioned sewers, a novelty in hospital construction. The water supply was derived from the main of the city. Barnes, *The Medical and Surgical History of the Civil War*, vol. 6: 949.

9. The first floor of the central building contained a dining hall that sat 1,200 people. The second floor of the central building contained a chapel and dormitories for female nurses. Barnes, *The Medical and Surgical History of the Civil War*, vol. 6: 949.

10. Behind the central building was a T-shaped building that was used as a general and extra diet kitchen and laundry. The bakery occupied separate rooms containing suitable ranges, steam fixtures, and bake ovens; and the laundry contained a system for steam drying. On the right of the projecting wards were buildings used as quarters for detail men, workshops, subsistence store-rooms, stable, wagon-house, and ward for contagious diseases; on the left were the knapsack and quartermaster's store rooms, sutler's stores, and some houses used as quarters by medical officers and stewards. Barnes, *The Medical and Surgical History of the Civil War*, vol. 6: 949.

11. To the right of the administration building was a building, 70 by 28 feet, which contained the linen room, post office, and officer's mess. Barnes, *The Medical and Surgical History of the Civil War*, vol. 6: 949.

12. To the left of the administration building was a building containing the dispensary, medical storerooms, room of the discharge board, and an operating room lighted from above. Barnes, *The Medical and Surgical History of the Civil War*, vol. 6: 949.

13. The guard-room and guard-house were also in front of the administration building, near the entrance to the hospital grounds. Barnes, *The Medical and Surgical History of the Civil War*, vol. 6: 949.

14. Erysipelas is a highly contagious streptococcal infection. There were relatively few cases of erysipelas arising in a traumatic wound, but when it did, the mortality rate was 41 percent. Its cause was a mystery, but it was clear that it spread easily through the air. Workers in a hospital in Louisville discovered that it could eliminate cases by spraying bromine vapor into the air. Adams, *Doctors in Blue*, 126.

15. Within the hospital culture there was a growing awareness of the effects of nutrition on healing. A lack of funding hampered hospitals' ability to meet the emerging dietary health challenges. After realizing the need for better food, Surgeon General Hammond drew up an experimental diet table that was tried for several months in 1862 in a number of hospitals. The results indicated faster recovery, but all the hospitals using the new diets went into debt. No relief could be had from Congress, so hospitals devised innovative methods to save money in other areas to extend the

NOTES TO PAGES 57–58

food budget. Gardens became commonplace, and civilian commissions worked endlessly to provide supplies beyond the army's budget. Adams, *Doctors in Blue*, 139. For more on medical care during the Civil War, see William Q. Maxwell, *Lincolns Fifth Wheel: The Political History of the United States Sanitary Commission* (New York: Longmans, Green, 1956); Glenna R. Schroeder-Lein, *Confederate Hospitals on the Move: Samuel H. Stout and the Army of Tennessee* (Columbia: University of South Carolina Press, 1994); George W. Smith, *Medicines for the Union Army: The United States Army Laboratories during the Civil War* (Madison, WI: American Institute of the History of Pharmacy, 1962); and Paul E. Steiner, *Disease in the Civil War: Natural Biological Warfare in 1861–1865* (Springfield, IL: C. C. Thomas, 1968).

16. As the medical community learned more about contagion, isolation hospitals began to emerge for specialized treatment of specific disease. In addition to the construction of infirmaries for patients with small pox, measles, and dysentery, special infirmaries were created for those that suffered from sexually transmitted diseases. The most common sexually transmitted diseases were syphilis and gonorrhea. At the time little was known about the various strains of other sexually transmitted diseases and therefore soldiers exhibiting the symptom of urethral discharge were diagnosed with gonorrhea. Syphilis was diagnosed in its primary and secondary forms. These forms manifested as superficial lesions on the skin or mucus membranes, often accompanied by general glandular enlargement. Through the course of the war 102,893 soldiers were diagnosed with gonorrhea and 79,589 soldiers were diagnosed with syphilis. Among white troops of the two groups 123 deaths were attributed to syphilis, and only 6 were linked to gonorrhea. It is difficult to know the exact number of deaths from syphilis because doctors did not yet understand the late stages of the disease, which attack the cardiovascular and central nervous system. Of the total diagnosed with either disease only 426 were treated in military hospitals. Bollet, *Civil War Medicine*, 307–25.

17. The Baltimore Alms House was created and overseen by the Trustees of the Poor of Baltimore County. In 1819 or 1820 this group purchased an estate known as "Calverton," the previous country seat of a gentleman by the name of Dennis J. Smith. The property was located about two-and-a-half miles from the court house on the Franklin Road and contained an elegant mansion to which the trustees added two additional wings to form the alms house. The alms house served as a hospital for the poor, an orphan asylum, and a home for mentally ill. It housed people with no obvious forms of support and over the course of its existence it doubled as a prison, a factory, and a workhouse until it burned down in 1875. Thomas Scharf, *The Chronicles of Baltimore: Being a Complete History of "Baltimore Town" and Baltimore City from the Earliest Period to the Present Time* (Baltimore, MD: Turnbull Brothers, 1874), 72–75.

18. In the early months of recruiting, pressure was high to fill quotas. Surgeons often gave recruits a superficial examination to increase the number of troops they approved for mustering in. This resulted in many diseased and infirm men entering the ranks of the army. Under these circumstances it is possible that Jack suffered from imbecility. It is also possible that he became psychotic after entering the war. Throughout the war, 2,410 white soldiers and 193 black soldiers were diagnosed as insane. Of these 869 white and 34 black soldiers were discharged on the basis of insanity. Bollet, Civil War Medicine, 260–65, 317–18.

19. As the war raged on and the casualty numbers increased, the presence of women employees in war hospitals became common. This proved to be an important event in American social history as hospital professions opened to women at a time when their economic options were limited. It is interesting to note that Maguire only mentions women nurses once-when he witnessed Clara Barton's arrival on the battlefield at Antietam. In August of 1861, Congress passed an act that allowed women to be substituted for men in general or permanent hospitals when the surgeon general or the surgeon in charge thought it necessary. In response thousands of women went to Washington with hopes of securing jobs as nurses. It is estimated that 3,200 women served as nurses throughout the war. The women who acted as nurses were not trained nurses as we understand them today, but their trials and tribulations while in the field laid the foundation for nursing school curricula to come. It is also interesting to note that the increased awareness of the power of diet to assist in recovery and healing was gendered in nature. Wartime activist Annie Wittenmyer oversaw the design, construction, and operation of multiple special diet kitchens in military hospitals across the country—for which she recruited and trained about two hundred female managers. Elizabeth D. Leonard, Yankee Women: Gender Battles in the Civil War (New York: W.W. Norton, 1994), 87; Adams, Doctors in Blue, 153–55.

20. Hick's United States General Hospital closed in June 1866. On Thursday October 4, 1866, at 11:00 a.m. the auction house of Adreon, Thomas and Co. auctioned off the buildings, fixtures, and appurtenances "known as Hicks' U.S. General Hospital." Consolidated Correspondence File for Hicks United States General Hospital located at the National Archives, Washington, DC. Record Number 928W210126, Box 807.

Conclusion

1. David Thelan, "Memory of American History," Journal of American History 75, no. 4 (Mar. 1989): 1117–29.
2. James M. McPherson, and William J. Cooper, eds., Writing the Civil War (Columbia: University of South Carolina Press, 1998), 6.
3. Fahs and Waugh. The Memory of the Civil War in American Culture, 2.

4. For more on the Grand Review, see George R. Sheets, *The Grand Review: The Civil War Continues to Shape America* (York, PA: Bold Print Inc., 2000) and Heidler, Heidler, and Coles, *Encyclopedia of the American Civil War.*

5. For more on commemoration and veterans following the war, see James A. Marten, *Sing Not War: The Lives of Union and Confederate Veterans in Gilded Age American* (Chapel Hill: University of North Carolina Press, 2011); James A. Marten, *America's Corporal: James Tanner in War and Peace* (Athens: University of Georgia Press, 2014); Keith M. Harris, *Across the Bloody Chasm: The Culture of Commemoration among Civil War Veterans* (Baton Rouge: Louisiana State University Press, 2014); and Brian Matthew Jordan, "Our Work is Not Yet Finished: Union Veterans and Their Unending Civil War, 1865–1872," *Journal of the Civil War Era* 5, no. 4 (2015): 484–503.

6. Dyer, *A Compendium of the War of Rebellion,* 1235.

7. 1870 U.S. Census, City of Baltimore, p. 123.

8. Wendy M. Duff and Catherine A. Johnson, "Where Is the List with All the Names? Information Seeking Behavior of Genealogists," *American Archivist* 66 (1) (Spring 2003): 79–95.

9. Elizabeth Yakel and Deborah A. Torres, "Genealogists as a 'Community of Records,'" *American Archivist* 70 (1) (2007): 93–113.

BIBLIOGRAPHY

Abels, Jules. *Man on Fire: John Brown and the Cause of Liberty*. New York: Macmillan, 1971.

Adams, George Worthington. *Doctors in Blue: the Medical History of the Union Army in the Civil War*. New York: H. Schuman, 1952.

Baker, Jean H. *The Politics of Continuity: Maryland Political Parties from 1858 to 1870*. Baltimore, MD: Johns Hopkins University Press, 1973.

The Baltimore Sun Historical Archives Headline: The Sun. The War News; Article Type: News/Opinion Paper: Sun, published as The Sun; Date: 09–17–1862; Volume: LI; Issue: 104; Page: [1]; Location: Baltimore, Maryland.

Bardaglio, Peter W. "The Children of Jubilee: African-American Childhood in Wartime," in *Divided Houses: Gender and the Civil War*, 213–29. Edited by Catherine Clinton and Nina Silber. New York and Oxford: Oxford University Press, 1992.

Barnes, Joseph K. *The Medical and Surgical History of the Civil War*. Wilmington, NC: Broadfoot, 1990.

Barton, Michael. *Good Men: The Character of Civil War Soldiers*. University Park, PA: Pennsylvania State University Press, 1981.

Barton, Michael, and Larry M. Logue, eds. *The Civil War Soldier: A Historical Reader*. New York: New York University Press, 2002.

Bennett, Michael J. *Union Jacks: Yankee Sailors in the Civil War*. Chapel Hill: University of North Carolina Press, 2004.

Bisbee, Saxon T. *Engines of Rebellion: Confederate Ironclads and Steam Engineering in the American Civil War*. Tuscaloosa: University of Alabama Press, 2018.

Blight, David W. *Race and Reunion: The Civil War in American Memory*. Cambridge, MA: Belknap Press of Harvard University Press, 2001.

Bollet, Alfred J. *Civil War Medicine Challenges and Triumphs*. Tucson, AZ: Galen Press, LTD, 2002.

Brasher, Glenn David. *The Peninsula Campaign and the Necessity of Emancipation: African Americans and the Fight for Freedom*. Chapel Hill, NC: University of North Carolina Press, 2012.

Brooks, Stewart M. *Civil War Medicine*. Springfield, IL: Thomas, 1966.

Brown, George William. *Baltimore and the Nineteenth of April, 1861: A Study of the War*. Baltimore, MD: Johns Hopkins University Press, 2001.

Brugger, Robert J. *Maryland, A Middle Temperament, 1634–1980*. Baltimore, MD: Johns Hopkins University Press in association with the Maryland Historical Society, 1988.

Brumgardt, John R., ed. Civil War Nurses: The Diary and Letters of Hannah Ropes. Knoxville: University of Tennessee Press, 1993.

Butchart, Ronald E. Schooling the Freed People: Teaching, Learning, and the Struggle for Black Freedom, 1861–1876. Chapel Hill: University of North Carolina Press, 2010.

Calore, Paul. Naval Campaigns of the Civil War. Jefferson, NC: McFarland, 2002.

Cannan, John. The Antietam Campaign August-September 1862. Conshohocken, PA: Combined Books, 1994.

Carmichael, Peter S. The War for the Common Soldier: How Men Thought, Fought, and Survived in Civil War Armies. Chapel Hill: University of North Carolina Press, 2018.

Clinton, Catherin. "Orphans of the Storm," in her Civil War Stories, 42–80. Athens and London: University of Georgia Press, 1998.

Cloyd, Benjamin G. Haunted by Atrocity: Civil War Prisons in American Memory. Baton Rouge: Louisiana State University Press, 2010.

Cooling, Benjamin Franklin, III. Counter-Thrust: From the Peninsula to the Antietam. Lincoln: University of Nebraska Press, 2007.

Cunningham, Horace H. Doctors in Grey. Baton Rouge: Louisiana State University Press, 1959.

Cutler, William G. History of the State of Kansas With Biographical Sketches and Portraits. Chicago: A. T. Andreas, 1883.

Daniels, Elizabeth. "The Children of Gettysburg," in American Heritage 40 (May–June 1989): 97–107.

Denney, Robert E. Civil War Medicine. New York: Sterling Publishers, 1994.

Denton, Lawrence M. A Southern Star for Maryland: Maryland and the Secession Crisis, 1860–1861. Baltimore: Publishing Concepts, 1995.

Donald, David, Jean Harvey Baker, and Michael F. Holt. The Civil War and Reconstruction. New York and London: Norton, 2001.

Donald, David Herbert, ed. Gone for a Soldier: The Civil War Memoirs of Private Alfred Bellard; from the Alec Thomas Archives. Boston: Little, Brown, 1975.

Dougherty, Kevin, and Michael Moore M.A. The Peninsula Campaign of 1862: A Military Analysis. Jackson: University Press of Mississippi, 2010.

Dowdy, Clifford. The Seven Days: The Emergence of Lee. Boston, MA: Little, Brown, 1974.

Drago, Edmund L. Confederate Phoenix: Rebel Children and their Families in South Carolina. New York: Fordham University Press, 2008.

Duff, Wendy M., and Catherine A. Johnson, "Where Is the List with All the Names? Information Seeking Behavior of Genealogists," American Archivist 66 (1) (Spring 2003): 79–95.

Dyer, Fredrick H. A Compendium of the War of the Rebellion. New York: T. Yoseloff, 1959.

Earle, Jonathan. John Brown's Raid on Harpers Ferry: A Brief History with Documents. Boston: Bedford/St. Martin's, 2008.

Eicher, John H., and David J. Eicher. *Civil War High Commands*. Stanford, CA: Stanford University Press, 2001.

Emerson, William K. *Encyclopedia of United States Army Insignia and Uniforms*. Norman: University of Oklahoma Press, 1996.

Ernst, Kathleen. *Too Afraid to Cry: Maryland Civilians in the Antietam Campaign*. Mechanicsburg, PA: Stackpole Books, 1999.

Ezratty, Harry A. *Baltimore in the Civil War: The Pratt Street Riot and a City Occupied*. Charleston: The History Press, 2010.

Fee, Elizabeth, Linda Shopes, and Linda Zeidman. *The Baltimore Book: New Views of Local History*. Philadelphia, PA: Temple University Press, 1991.

Fowler, William M., *Under Two Flags: The American Navy in the Civil War*. New York: Norton, 2001.

Freeman, Douglas S. *R. E. Lee: A Biography*. New York; London: C. Scribner's Sons, 1934.

Freemon, Frank R. *Gangrene and Glory: Medical Care during the Civil War*. Rutherford: Fairleigh Dickinson University Press, 1999.

———. Microbes and Minie Balls: An Annotated Bibliography of Civil War Medicine. Rutherford: Fairleigh Dickinson University Press, 1993.

Frye, Dennis E. *Antietam Revealed: The Battle of Antietam and the Maryland Campaign as You Have Never Seen It Before*. Collingwood, NJ: C.W. Historicals, 2004.

———. Harpers Ferry Nestled Between North and South. Harrisburg, PA: Weider History Group, 2008.

———. Harpers Ferry Under Fire: A Border Town in the American Civil War. Brookfield, MO: Donning Company Publishers, 2011.

Fuller, Howard J. *Clad in Iron: The American Civil War and the Challenge of British Naval Power*. Westport, CT: Praeger Security International, 1968 and 2008.

Gallagher, Gary W., ed. *Antietam: Essays on the 1862 Maryland Campaign*. Kent, OH: Kent State University Press, 1989.

———, ed. The Antietam Campaign: Military Campaigns of the Civil War. Chapel Hill: University of North Carolina Press, 1999.

———, ed. The Richmond Campaign of 1862: The Peninsula and the Seven Days. Chapel Hill, NC: University of North Carolina Press, 2000.

Glatthaar, Joseph T. *The March to the Sea and Beyond: Sherman's Troops in the Savannah and Carolinas Campaigns*. Baton Rouge: Louisiana State University Press, 1995.

Glymph, Thavolia. "Noncombatant Military Laborers in the Civil War." *OAH Magazine of History* 26(2) (2012): 25–29.

Goodwin, Doris Kearns. *Team of Rivals: The Political Genius of Abraham Lincoln*. New York: Simon and Schuster, 2005.

Grunder, Charles S., and Brandon H. Beck. *The Second Battle of Winchester, June 12–15, 1863: The Virginia Civil War Battles and Leaders Series*. Lynchburg, VA: H. E. Howard, 1989.

Hahn, Thomas F. *The Chesapeake and Ohio Canal: Pathway to the Nation's Capital.* Metuchen, NJ: Scarecrow Press, Inc., 1984.

Harris, M. Keith. *Across the Bloody Chasm: The Culture of Commemoration among Civil War Veterans.* Baton Rouge: Louisiana State University Press, 2014.

Harsh, Joseph. *Confederate Tide Rising: Robert E. Lee and the Making of Southern Strategy, 1961–1862.* Kent, OH: Kent State University Press, 1998.

———. *Taken at the Flood: Robert E. Lee and Confederate Strategy in the Maryland Campaign of 1862.* Kent, OH: Kent State University Press, 1998.

Hartwig, D. Scott. *To Antietam Creek: The Maryland Campaign of September 1862.* Baltimore, MD: Johns Hopkins University Press, 2012.

Hartzler, Daniel D. *Marylanders in the Confederacy.* Westminster, MD: Family Line Publications, 1986.

Harwell, Richard B. *Kate: The Journal of a Confederate Nurse.* Baton Rouge: Louisiana State University Press, 1959.

Hassler, Warren W. *General George B. McClellan: Shield of the Union.* Baton Rouge: Louisiana State University Press, 1957.

Hattaway, Herman. *Shades of Blue and Grey.* Columbia: University of Missouri Press, 1991.

Hearn, Chester G. *Six Years of Hell: Harpers Ferry During the Civil War.* Baton Rouge: Louisiana State University Press, 1996.

Heidler, David Stephen, Jeanne T. Heidler, and David J. Coles. *Encyclopedia of the American Civil War: A Political, Social and Military History.* Santa Barbara, CA: ABC-CLIO, 2000.

Hess, Earl J. *Liberty, Virtue, and Progress: Northerners and Their War for the Union.* New York: New York University Press, 1988.

———. *The Union Soldier in Battle: Enduring the Ordeal of Combat.* Lawrence: University Press of Kansas, 1997.

Hesseltine, William Best. *Civil War Prisons.* Kent, OH: Kent State University Press, 1972.

Holloway, Anna Gibson, and Jonathan W. White. *"Our Little Monitor": The Greatest Invention of the Civil War.* Kent, OH: The Kent State University Press, 2018.

Jabour, Anya. *Topsy-Turvy: How the Civil War Turned the World Upside Down for Southern Children.* Chicago: Ivan R. Dee, 2010.

Janney, Caroline E. *Remembering the Civil War: Reunion and the Limits of Reconciliation.* Chapel Hill: University of North Carolina Press, 2013.

Jordan, Brian Matthew *Unholy Sabbath: The Battle of South Mountain in History and Memory: September 14, 1862.* New York: Savas Beatie, 2012.

———. *"Our Work is Not Yet Finished: Union Veterans and Their Unending Civil War, 1865–1872." Journal of the Civil War Era* 5, no. 4 (2015): 484–503.

Jones, Ray. *Harpers Ferry.* Gretna, LA: Pelican, 1992.

Konstam, Angus. *Fair Oaks 1862: McClellan's Peninsula Campaign.* Westport, CT: Praeger, 2004.

Korn, Bertram Wallace. *American Jewry and the Civil War*. Philadelphia, PA: The Jewish Publication Society of America, 1951.

Leepson, Marc. *The Flag: An American Biography*. New York: Thomas Dunn Books/St Martin's Press, 2005.

Leonard, Elizabeth D. *Yankee Women: Gender Battles in the Civil War*. New York: W.W. Norton, 1994.

Linderman, Gerald F. *Embattled Courage: The Experience of Combat in the American Civil War*. New York; London: Free Press, 1987.

Manakee, Harold R. *Maryland in the Civil War*. Baltimore: Maryland Historical Society, 1961.

Marten, James A. *America's Corporal: James Tanner in War and Peace*. Athens: University of Georgia Press, 2014.

Marten, James A. *Children and Youth during the Civil War Era*. New York: New York University Press, 2012.

———. *Children for the Union: The War Spirit on the Northern Home Front*. Chicago: Ivan R. Dee, 2004.

———. "Fatherhood in the Confederacy: Southern Soldiers and Their Children," *Journal of Southern History* 63 (May 1997): 269–92.

———."For the Good, the True, and the Beautiful: Northern Children's Magazines and the Civil War," *Civil War History* 41 (Mar. 1995): 57–75.

———. *Lessons of War: The Civil War in Children's Magazines*. Wilmington, DE: SR Books, 1999.

———. *Sing Not War: The Lives of Union and Confederate Veterans in Gilded Age American*. Chapel Hill: University of North Carolina Press, 2011.

———. "Stern Realities: Children of Chancellorsville and Beyond," in *Chancellorsville: The Battle and Its Aftermath*, 219–43. Edited by Gary W. Gallagher. Chapel Hill and London: University of North Carolina Press, 1996.

Maryland State Archives, 350 Rowe Boulevard, Annapolis, MD 21401

Maxwell, William Q. *Lincolns Fifth Wheel: The Political History of the United States Sanitary Commission*. New York: Longmans, Green, 1956.

McPherson, James M. *For Cause and Comrades: Why Men Fought in the Civil War*. New York: Oxford University Press, 1997.

———. *Marching Toward Freedom: The Negro in the Civil War*. New York: Knopf, 1967.

———. *The Negro's Civil War: How American Negroes Felt and Acted During the War for the Union*. New York: Pantheon Books, 1965.

———. *Ordeal by Fire: The Civil War and Reconstruction*. New York: Knopf, 1982.

———. *War on the Waters: The Union and Confederate Navies, 1861–1865*. Chapel Hill: University of North Carolina Press, 2012.

McPherson, James M., and William J. Cooper, eds. *Writing the Civil War: The Quest to Understand*. Columbia: University of South Carolina Press, 1998.

Meir, Kathryn Shively. *Nature's Civil War: Common Soldiers and the Environment in 1862 Virginia*. Chapel Hill: University of North Carolina Press, 2014.

Miller, Brian Craig. *John Bell Hood and the Fight for Civil War Memory.* Knoxville: University of Tennessee Press, 2010.

Miller, William J., ed. *The Peninsula Campaign of 1862: Yorktown to the Seven Days,* vol. 2. Boston, MA: Da Capo Press, 1995.

Mintz, Steven. *Huck's Raft: A History of American Childhood.* Cambridge, MA: Belknap Press of Harvard University Press, 2004.

Mitchell, Reid. *Civil War Soldiers.* New York, NY: Viking, 1988.

Murfin, James. *The Gleam of Bayonets: the battle of Antietam and the Maryland Campaign of 1862.* Baton Rouge, LA: Louisiana State University Press, 1982.

Murphy, Jim. *The Boys' War: Confederate and Union Soldiers Talk about the Civil War.* New York: Clarion Books, 1990.

Musicant, Ivan. *Divided Waters: The Naval History of the Civil War.* New York: Harper Collins Publishers, 1995.

Nash, Howard P. *A Naval History of the Civil War.* South Brunswick: A. S. Barnes, 1972.

Oates, Stephen B. *A Woman of Valor: Clara Barton and the Civil War.* New York: Free Press, 1994.

Ott, Victoria E. *Confederate Daughters: Coming of Age during the Civil War.* Carbondale: Southern Illinois University Press, 2008.

Palfrey, Francis. *The Antietam and Fredericksburg.* New York: Charles Scribner's Sons, 1882.

Pfanz, Donald C. *Clara Barton's Civil War: Between Bullet and Hospital.* Yardley, PA: Westholme, 2018.

Porter, David D. *The Naval History of the Civil War.* Secaucus, NJ: Castle, 1984.

Pumroy, Eric, and Katja Rampelmann. *Research Guide to the Turner Movement in the United States.* Bibliographies and Indexes in American History, no. 33. Westport, CT: Greenwood Press, 1996.

Rafuse, Ethan S. *Antietam, South Mountain, and Harpers Ferry.* Lincoln: University of Nebraska Press, 2008.

———. *McClellan's' War: The Failure of Moderation in the Struggle for the Union.* Bloomington Indiana University Press, 2005.

Reid, Richard M. *Freedom for Themselves: North Carolina's Black Soldiers in the Civil War Era.* Chapel Hill: University of North Carolina Press, 2008.

Roberts, William H. *Civil War Ironclads: The U.S. Navy and Industrial Mobilization.* Baltimore, MD: Johns Hopkins University Press, 2007.

Robertson, James I. Jr. *Soldiers Blue and Grey.* Columbia: University of South Carolina Press, 1988.

Roland, Charles Pierce. *An American Iliad: The Story of the Civil War.* Lexington: University Press of Kentucky, 1991.

Rosen, Robert N. *The Jewish Confederates.* Columbia: University of South Carolina Press, 2000.

Ross, Ishbell. *Angel of the Battlefield: The Life of Clara Barton.* New York: Harper, 1956.

Rubin, Anne Sarah. *Through the Heart of Dixie: Sherman's March and American Memory*. Chapel Hill: University of North Carolina Press, 2014.

Sarna, Jonathan D. *Jews and the Civil War: A Reader*. New York: New York University Press, 2010.

———. *Lincoln and the Jews: A History*. New York: Thomas Dunne Books/St. Martin's Press, 2015.

Scharf, Thomas. *The Chronicles of Baltimore Being a Complete History of Baltimore Town and Baltimore City From the Earliest Period to the Present Time*. Baltimore, MD: Turnbull Brothers, 1874.

Schroeder, Rudolph J. III. *Seven Days before Richmond: McClellan's Peninsula Campaign of 1862 and its Aftermath*. Bloomington, IN: iUniverse Press: 2009.

Schroeder-Lein, Glenna R. *Confederate Hospitals on the Move: Samuel H. Stout and the Army of Tennessee*. Columbia: University of South Carolina Press, 1994.

Scott, Rebecca J. "The Battle over the Child: Child Apprenticeship and the Freedmen's Bureau in North Carolina," in *Growing Up in America: Children in Historical Perspective*, 193–207. Edited by. N. Ray Hiner and Joseph M. Hawes. Urbana: University of Illinois Press, 1985.

Scott, Robert N., H.M Lazelle, George Davis, Leslie J. Perry, Joseph W. Kirkley, Fred C. Ainsworth, John S. Moodey, Calvin D. Cowles. *The War of the Rebellion: A Compilation of the Official Records of the Union and Confederate Armies*. Washington: Government Printing Office, 1880.

Sears, Stephen W. *George B. McClellan: The Young Napoleon*. New York, NY: Ticknor & Fields, 1988.

———. *Landscape Turned Red: The Battle of Antietam*. Boston, MA, and New York: Houghton Mifflin, 1983.

———. *To the Gates of Richmond: The Peninsula Campaign*. New York: Ticknor & Fields, 1992.

Sheads, Scott Sumpter, and Daniel Carroll Toomey. *Baltimore during the Civil War*. Linthicum, MD: Toomey Press, 1997.

Sheehan-Dean, Aaron Charles. *The View from the Ground: Experiences of Civil War Soldiers*. Lexington: University Press of Kentucky, 2007.

Sheets, George R. *The Grand Review: The Civil War Continues to Shape America*. York, PA.: Bold Print2000.

Simonoff, Harry. *Jewish Participants in the Civil War*. New York: Arco Publishing Company Inc., 1963.

Smith, George W. *Medicines for the Union Army: The United States Army Laboratories During the Civil War*. Madison, WI: American Institute of the History of Pharmacy, 1962.

Smith, John David, ed. *Black Soldiers in Blue: African American Troops in the Civil War Era*. Chapel Hill: University of North Carolina Press, 2002.

Smith, Myron J. *American Civil War Navies: A Bibliography*, vol. 3. Metuchen, NJ: Scarecrow Press, 1972.

Steers, Edward. *The Trial: The Assassination of President Lincoln and the Trial of the Conspirators*. Lexington: University Press of Kentucky, 2003.

Steiner, Paul E. *Disease in the Civil War: Natural Biological Warfare in 1861–1865*. Springfield, IL: C. C. Thomas, 1968.

Symonds, Craig L. *The Civil War at Sea*. Santa Barbara, CA: Praeger, 2009.

———. *Confederate Admiral: The Life and Wars of Franklin Buchanan*. Annapolis, Md.: Naval Institute Press, 1999.

———. *The Civil War at Sea*. Santa Barbara, CA: Praeger, 2009.

———. *Union Combined Operations in the Civil War*. New York: Fordham University Press, 2010.

Symonds, Craig L., and Thomas B. Buell. *Decision at Sea: Five Naval Battles that Shaped American History*. New York, Oxford: Oxford University Press, 2005.

Taaffe, Stephen R. *Commanding Lincoln's Navy: Union Naval Leadership during the Civil War*. Annapolis, Md: Naval Institute Press, 2009.

Tanner, Robert G. *Stonewall in the Valley: Thomas J. "Stonewall" Jackson's Shenandoah Valley Campaign, Spring 1862*. Garden City, NY: Doubleday, 1976.

Thelan, David. *Memory and American History*. Bloomington: Indiana University Press, 1990.

Toomey, Daniel Carroll. *The Civil War in Maryland*. Baltimore, MD: Toomey Press, 1983.

———. "Gilmore's Raid." Lecture, Jerusalem Mill Village Kingsville MD, July 11, 2009.

United States. Naval History Division. *Civil War Naval Chronology 1861–1865*. Washington: U.S. G.P.O, 1971. Compiled by the U.S. War Department, Office of the Surgeon General. *The Medical and Surgical History of the War of Rebellion*, 6 vols. (1875–1888).

Varle, Charles. *A Complete View of Baltimore With a Statistical Sketch of all the Commercial, Mercantile, Manufacturing, Literary, Scientific, and Religious Institutions and Establishments, In the Same, and In Its Vicinity for Fifteen Miles Round, Derived from Personal Observation and Research Into the Most Authentic Sources of Information*. Baltimore: S. Young, 1833.

Waugh, Joan, *The Memory of the Civil War in American Culture*. Chapel Hill: University of North Carolina Press, 2004.

Werner, Emily E. *Reluctant Witnesses: Children's Voices from the Civil War*. New York: Westview Press, 1998.West, Richard S. *Lincoln's Scapegoat General: A life of Benjamin F. Butler, 1818–1893*. Boston: Houghton Mifflin, 1965.

Wheelan, Joseph. *Libby Prison Breakout: The Daring Escape from the Notorious Civil War Prison*. New York: Public Affairs, 2010.

Wiley, Bell Irvin. *The Common Soldier in the Civil War*. New York NY: Grosset & Dunlap, 1958.

———. *The Life of Billy Yank: the Common Soldier of the Union*. Garden City, N.Y.: Doubleday, 1971.

————. *The Life of Johnny Reb: the Common Soldier of the Confederacy*. Garden City, N.Y.: Doubleday, 1943.

Williams, Blanche Colton. *Clara Barton, Daughter of Destiny*. Philadelphia and New York: J.B. Lippincott Company, 1941.

Wood, Ann Douglas. "The War Within a War: Women Nurses in the Union Army," *Civil War History*, 09/1972, Volume 18, Issue 3.

Yakel, Elizabeth, and Deborah A. Torres. "Genealogists as a 'Community of Records,'" *American Archivist* 70 (1) (2007): 93–113.

INDEX

Shenandoah River, 39, 40, 84n1,
     87n11
Sibley tent, 16–17, 75n13
South Mountain, Battle of, xxii, 28,
     78n4, 79nn8–9, 84n1

Turner Society, 16, 75n12
Turners Gap, xxii

uniform buttons, 16, 74n10
Union army, xx, 5, 62, 70n14, 81n18,
     82nn19–20, 88n4
Union Jack, 15

Washington, DC, 2, 24, 25, 31, 45, 60,
     67n2, 68n8, 69n13, 70n16, 71n17,
     71n1, 74n9, 77n24, 77n1, 78n4,
     79n8, 82n20, 84n1, 86n8, 92n19
Winchester, xxiv, 49, 62, 87n11,
     87n13